Editors
Tracy Edmunds, M.A.
Sara Connolly

Managing Editor
Ina Massler Levin, M.A.

Illustrator
Sue Fullam

Cover Artist
Brenda DiAntonis

Art Production Manager
Kevin Barnes

Art Coordinator
Renée Christine Yates

Imaging
Rosa C. See

Publisher
Mary D. Smith, M.S. Ed.

Author

Susan Mackey Collins, M.Ed.

Teacher Created Resources, Inc.
12621 Western Avenue
Garden Grove, CA 92841
www.teachercreated.com

ISBN: 978-1-4206-3958-2

©*2006 Teacher Created Resources, Inc.*
Reprinted, 2020
Made in U.S.A.

Table of Contents

Introduction

The wealth of knowledge a person gains throughout his or her lifetime is impossible to measure, and it will certainly vary from person to person. However, regardless of the scope of knowledge, the foundation for all learning remains a constant. All that we know and think throughout our lifetimes is based upon fundamentals, and these fundamentals are the basic skills upon which all learning develops. *Mastering Third Grade Skills* is a book that reinforces a variety of third grade basic skills.

- **Writing**
- **Grammar**
- **Literature**
- **Math**
- **Social Studies**
- **Science**

This book was written with the wide range of student skills and ability levels of third grade students in mind. Both teachers and parents can benefit from the variety of pages provided in this book. Parents can use the book to provide an introduction to new material or to reinforce material already familiar to their children. Similarly, teachers can select pages that provide additional practice for concepts taught in the classroom. When tied to what is being covered in class, pages from this book make great homework reinforcement. The worksheets provided in this book are ideal for use at home as well as in the classroom. Research shows us that skill mastery comes with exposure and drill. To be internalized, concepts must be reviewed until they become second nature. Parents may certainly foster the classroom experience by exposing their children to the necessary skills whenever possible, and teachers will find that these pages perfectly complement their classroom needs. An answer key, beginning on page 224, provides teachers, parents, and children with a quick method of checking responses to completed work sheets.

Basic skills are utilized every day in untold ways. Make the practice of them part of your children's or students' routines. Such work done now will benefit them in countless ways throughout their lives.

Meeting Standards

Each lesson in Mastering Third Grade Skills meets one or more of the following standards, which are used with permission from McREL (Copyright 2000 McRel, Mid-continent Research for Education and Learning. Telephone: 303-337-0990. Website: *www.mcrel.org.*)

Language Arts Standards	Page Number
• Writes in cursive	8–33
• Uses exclamatory and imperative sentences in written composition	34–35
• Uses pronouns in written compositions	33–35
• Uses nouns in written compositions	34–38
• Uses verbs in written compositions	39–45
• Uses adjectives in written compositions	50–51
• Uses adverbs in written compositions	52–53
• Uses conventions of capitalization in written composition	54–58
• Uses conventions of punctuation in written composition	59–60
• Understands the ways in which language is used in literary texts	69–74
• Makes inferences or draws conclusions about characters' qualities and actions	76, 78
• Understands the basic concepts of setting and cause and effect	75, 77

Mathematics Standards	Page Number
• Adds, subtracts, multiplies, and divides whole numbers and decimals	79–109
• Solves simple open sentences involving operations on whole numbers	84, 92
• Adds and subtracts simple fractions	111–116
• Understands the properties of and the relationships among addition, subtraction, multiplication, and division	94–105
• Solves real-world problems involving number operations	117–119
• Recognizes a wide variety of patterns	120–121
• Selects and uses appropriate tools for given measurement situations	122–123
• Understands relationships between measures	127
• Understands and applies basic and advanced properties of the concepts of measurement	124–128

Meeting Standards (cont.)

Mathematics Standards (cont)	Page Number
• Understands the basic measures perimeter, area and angle	129–130, 135
• Knows basic geometric language for describing and naming shapes	128–130
• Understands characteristics of plane figures and lines	131–134
• Understands the concepts of congruence and symmetry	136–139
• Tells time to five minutes	140–143
• Reads and interprets simple bar graphs and tally marks	146–148

Social Studies Standards	Page Number
• Understands time in years, decades, and centuries	149
• Knows how to interpret data presented in time lines	150–152
• Knows how to construct time lines	152
• Distinguishes between past, present, and future time	153–155
• Understands family life now and in the past, and family life in various places long ago	152
• Knows how to identify patterns of change and continuity	154
• Understands the interactions that occurred between the Native Americans or Hawaiians and the first European, African, and Asian-Pacific explorers and settlers in the state or region	158, 166
• Understands how people in the local community have displayed courage in helping the common good	157
• Understands the historical events and democratic values commemorated by major national holidays	158
• Understands various aspects of family life, structures, and roles in different cultures and in many eras	159
• Understands the historical development and daily life of a colonial community	162
• Understands the challenges and difficulties encountered by people in pioneer farming communities	164-165
• Knows about the forced relocation of Native Americans and how their lives, rights, and territories were affected by European colonization and expansion of the U.S.	169

Meeting Standards *(cont.)*

Social Studies Standards *(cont)*	Page Number
• Understands how regional folk heroes and other popular figures have contributed to the cultural history of the U.S.	170
• Understands the effects geography has had on different aspects of societies	171
• Understands the basic ideas set forth in the Declaration of Independence and the U.S. Constitution, and the figures responsible for these documents	172–174
• Understands how songs, symbols, and slogans demonstrate freedom of expression and the role of protest in a democracy	174–176, 179–180
• Knows the Pledge of Allegiance and patriotic songs, poems, and sayings that were written long ago, and understands their significance	177
• Understands the basic principles of American democracy	180
• Understands how people over the last 200 years have continued to struggle to bring to all groups in American society the liberties and equality promised in the basic principles of American democracy	181–182
• Understands the people, events, problems, and ideas that were significant in creating the history of their state	183–186
• Knows about the first inhabitants who lived in the state or region, what their lives were like, and their experiences of adjustment	186

Science Standards	Page Number
• Knows that plants and animals progress through life cycles of birth, growth and development, reproduction, and death; the details of these life cycles are different for different organisms	187, 191
• Knows that behavior of individual organisms is influenced by internal cues and external cues, and that humans and other organisms have senses that help them to detect these cues	188
• Knows that living organisms have distinct structures and body systems that serve specific functions in growth, survival, and reproduction	189, 190
• Knows that many characteristics of an organism are inherited from its parents, and other characteristics result from an individual's interactions with the environment	192

Meeting Standards (cont.)

Science Standards (cont)	Page Number
• Knows that the transfer of energy is essential to all living organisms	193, 195, 196
• Knows the organization of simple food chains and food webs	194
• Knows that all organisms cause changes in their environments, and these changes can be beneficial or detrimental	198
• Knows that rock is composed of different combinations of minerals	199–200
• Knows the composition and properties of soils	198
• Knows that fossils provide evidence about the plants and animals that lived long ago and the nature of the environment at that time	203
• Knows that water exists in the air in different forms	204
• Knows that night and day are caused by the Earth's rotation on its axis	206–207
• Knows that the Earth is one of several planets that orbit the Sun and that the Moon orbits the Earth	208–212
• Knows that the Earth's gravity pulls any object toward it without touching it	213
• Knows the relationship between the strength of a force and its effect on an object	214
• Knows that when a force is applied to an object, the object either speeds up, slows down, or goes in a different direction	215, 216
• Knows that magnets attract and repel each other and attract certain kinds of other materials	217
• Knows that matter has different states and that each state has distinct physical properties; some common materials such as water can be changed from one state to another by heating or cooling	219–220
• Knows that the mass of a material remains constant whether it is together, in parts, or in a different state	221

A is for Apple

$\mathcal{A}$ a

Directions: Trace each cursive letter and word. Write each letter four times. Practice writing each word.

a   *a*

a   *a*

a   *a*

a   *a*

Apple

Apple

apple

apple

B is for Banana

Directions: Trace each cursive letter and word. Write each letter four times. Practice writing each word.

$\mathcal{B}$ $\mathcal{B}$

$\mathcal{B}$ $\mathcal{B}$

b   *b*

b   *b*

Banana

Banana

banana

banana

C is for Cat

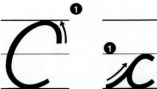

Directions: Trace each cursive letter and word. Write each letter four times. Practice writing each word.

C C

C C

c c

c c

Cat

Cat

cat

cat

D is for Dog

Directions: Trace each cursive letter and word. Write each letter four times. Practice writing each word.

D   *D*

D   *D*

d   *d*

d   *d*

Dog

Dog

dog

dog

E is for Elephant

Directions: Trace each cursive letter and word. Write each letter four times. Practice writing each word.

$\mathcal{E}$ .... $\mathcal{E}$

$\mathcal{E}$ .... $\mathcal{E}$

$\mathcal{e}$ .... $\mathcal{e}$

$\mathcal{e}$ .... $\mathcal{e}$

Elephant

Elephant

elephant

elephant

F is for Frog

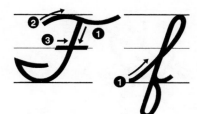

Directions: Trace each cursive letter and word. Write each letter four times. Practice writing each word.

F   *F*

F   *F*

f   *f*

f   *f*

Frog

Frog

frog

frog

G is for Gerbil

Directions: Trace each cursive letter and word. Write each letter four times. Practice writing each word.

$\mathcal{G}$ $\mathcal{G}$

$\mathcal{G}$ $\mathcal{G}$

g g

g g

Gerbil

Gerbil

gerbil

gerbil

H is for Hat

Directions: Trace each cursive letter and word. Write each letter four times. Practice writing each word.

H   H

H   H

h   h

h   h

Hat

Hat

hat

hat

I is for Igloo

I   i

Directions: Trace each cursive letter and word. Write each letter four times. Practice writing each word.

I   *I*

I   *I*

i   *i*

i   *i*

Igloo

Igloo

igloo

igloo

J is for Jam

Directions: Trace each cursive letter and word. Write each letter four times. Practice writing each word.

J   *J*

J   *J*

j   *j*

j   *j*

Jam

Jam

jam

jam

K is for Ketchup

Directions: Trace each cursive letter and word. Write each letter four times. Practice writing each word.

𝒦   𝒦

𝒦   𝒦

𝓀   𝓀

𝓀   𝓀

Ketchup

Ketchup

ketchup

ketchup

L is for Lion

①

$$\mathscr{L} \cdot \ell$$

Directions: Trace each cursive letter and word. Write each letter four times. Practice writing each word.

$\mathscr{L}$ $\mathscr{L}$

$\mathscr{L}$ $\mathscr{L}$

ℓ ℓ

ℓ ℓ

Lion

Lion

lion

lion

M is for Mouse

$\mathcal{M}$ · m

Directions: Trace each cursive letter and word. Write each letter four times. Practice writing each word.

$\mathcal{M}$ $\mathcal{M}$

$\mathcal{M}$ $\mathcal{M}$

m m

m m

Mouse

Mouse

mouse

mouse

N is for Noodle

$\mathcal{N}$ · $\mathcal{m}$

Directions: Trace each cursive letter and word. Write each letter four times. Practice writing each word.

$\mathcal{N}$ $\mathcal{N}$

$\mathcal{N}$ $\mathcal{N}$

$\mathcal{n}$ $\mathcal{n}$

$\mathcal{n}$ $\mathcal{n}$

Noodle

Noodle

noodle

noodle

O is for Octopus

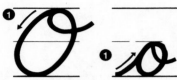

Directions: Trace each cursive letter and word. Write each letter four times. Practice writing each word.

O O

O O

o o

o o

Octopus

Octopus

octopus

octopus

P is for Pizza

Directions: Trace each cursive letter and word. Write each letter four times. Practice writing each word.

P   P

P   P

p   p

p   p

Pizza

Pizza

pizza

pizza

Q is for Quarter

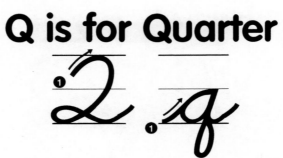

Directions: Trace each cursive letter and word. Write each letter four times. Practice writing each word.

2   *2*

2   *2*

q   *q*

q   *q*

Quarter

Quarter

quarter

quarter

R is for Rabbit

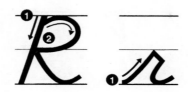

Directions: Trace each cursive letter and word. Write each letter four times. Practice writing each word.

R R

R R

r r

r r

Rabbit

Rabbit

rabbit

rabbit

S for Snowman

Directions: Trace each cursive letter and word. Write each letter four times. Practice writing each word.

S   *S*

S   *S*

s   *s*

s   *s*

Snowman

Snowman

snowman

snowman

T is for Tree

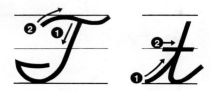

Directions: Trace each cursive letter and word. Write each letter four times. Practice writing each word.

$\mathcal{T}$ $\mathcal{T}$

$\mathcal{T}$ $\mathcal{T}$

t t

t t

Tree

Tree

tree

tree

U is for Unicorn

$\mathcal{U}$ $\mathcal{u}$

Directions: Trace each cursive letter and word. Write each letter four times. Practice writing each word.

$\mathcal{U}$ $\mathcal{U}$

$\mathcal{U}$ $\mathcal{U}$

$\mathcal{u}$ $\mathcal{u}$

$\mathcal{u}$ $\mathcal{u}$

Unicorn

Unicorn

unicorn

unicorn

V is for Violin

Directions: Trace each cursive letter and word. Write each letter four times. Practice writing each word.

W is for World

Directions: Trace each cursive letter and word. Write each letter four times. Practice writing each word.

$\mathcal{W}$ $\mathcal{W}$

$\mathcal{W}$ $\mathcal{W}$

w w

w w

$\mathcal{W}orld$

$\mathcal{W}orld$

$world$

$world$

X is for X-ray

Directions: Trace each cursive letter and word. Write each letter four times. Practice writing each word.

$\mathcal{X}$ $\mathcal{X}$

$\mathcal{X}$ $\mathcal{X}$

x x

x x

$\mathcal{X}$-ray

$\mathcal{X}$-ray

x-ray

x-ray

Y is for Yo Yo

$\mathcal{Y}$ y

Directions: Trace each cursive letter and word. Write each letter four times. Practice writing each word.

$\mathcal{Y}$ $\mathcal{Y}$

$\mathcal{Y}$ $\mathcal{Y}$

y y

y y

Yo-yo

Yo-yo

yo-yo

yo-yo

Z is for Zebra

Directions: Trace each cursive letter and word. Write each letter four times. Practice writing each word.

How Exciting!

An *exclamatory* sentence shows excitement or emotion.

How great our field trip was!

Directions: Read each question. Write an exclamatory sentence to answer each question.

Example: Can you believe you had a surprise party?

　　　　　　Gosh, the party was a total surprise to me!

1. Did you have a good birthday? _____

   _____

2. What was your favorite present? _____

   _____

3. Were the clowns funny?_____

   _____

4. How fun was your party _____

   _____

5. Did everyone have a good time at the party? _____

   _____

6. How much cake and ice cream did you eat? _____

   _____

Simon Says

In the game Simon Says everyone has to obey Simon's commands. An *imperative* or *command* sentence is a lot like Simon. This type of sentence tells or asks someone to do something.

Examples: Please, sit down.

Sit down now.

Directions: Read each sentence. If the sentence is a command, write the letter C on the line.

1. Go to the office. _____

2. How wonderful you look! _____

3. Sit next to me. _____

4. Answer the phone. _____

5. Do you know my name? _____

6. Give me more dessert. _____

7. Chocolate pie is delicious. _____

8. Get ready to go. _____

9. I love you. _____

10. Answer the next question. _____

Being Agreeable

A *pronoun* is a word that takes the place of a noun. A pronoun must match in number and gender the noun that it replaces.

Examples: Karen is my friend.

She is very nice.

You wouldn't write *he is nice* because Karen is a girl, not a boy.

Part I

Directions: Circle the correct pronoun in each sentence.

1. Jake lost (his, her) notebook.

2. The family is going on vacation because (they, it) want to visit Florida.

3. My mother bought a diamond ring and she put it in (his, her) safe.

4. The children went to the movies, and (it, they) bought a lot of popcorn to eat.

5. Sally gave (her, its) parents a gift for their anniversary.

Part II

Directions: Circle the words that are pronouns.

candy	he	dog
she	week	chair
it	they	you
me	little	I
to	us	we

Match Them Up

A *pronoun* is a word that takes the place of a noun.

Directions: Match each pronoun piece to the correct noun piece by coloring both pieces the same color.

Pronouns   Nouns

he

sunshine

she

Mandy

it

Brett, Sadie, and Gage

we

Joan and I

they

Jack

It Was a Dark and Stormy Night

Directions: Use a least 10 pronouns to finish the story below. In your story, circle each pronoun you use.

he	she	it	they
us	we	her	him
you	me	them	I

It was a dark and stormy night, and I was home alone. My parents had gone to dinner and had decided to leave me by myself for the very first time. Everything was going great until I heard a noise in the basement. The next thing I knew...

_____

_____

_____

_____

_____

_____

_____

_____

_____

_____

_____

_____

Name That Picture

A *noun* that is singular names one person, place, or thing.

Directions: Look at each picture. On the lines provided, write the singular noun that names each picture.

1.

_____

2.

_____

3.

_____

4.

_____

5.

_____

6.

_____

7.

_____

8.

_____

9.

_____

10.

_____

Just Add an SSSSS

To make a noun plural, you usually add the letter *S*.

Directions: Change each noun to a plural noun by adding the letter *S*. Write the new word on the line provided.

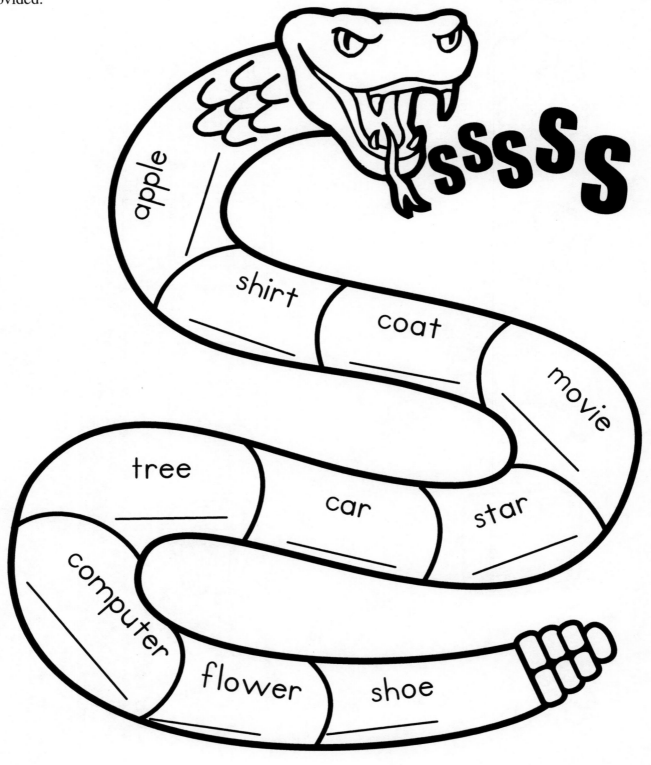

Singular or Plural?

A *singular noun* names one person, place, or thing.

A *plural noun* names more than one person, place, or thing.

Part I

Directions: Look at the singular nouns in the word bank. Write a sentence using each of these nouns.

> cat   house   book   ball

1. _____
   _____
2. _____
   _____
3. _____
   _____
4. _____
   _____

Part II

Directions: Look at the plural nouns in the word bank. Write a sentence using each of these nouns.

> kids   teams   pizzas   students

1. _____
   _____
2. _____
   _____
3. _____
   _____
4. _____
   _____

Something Different

Most nouns become plural by adding the letter *s* or *es*. However, some nouns need different endings.

cherry   cherries

child   children

mouse   mice

Directions: Write the plural form of each noun.

1. goose _____

2. story _____

3. man_____

4. ox _____

5. leaf _____

6. berry_____

7. lady_____

8. deer_____

9. penny _____

10. woman _____

Proper and Common

A proper noun is always capitalized. *A common noun* is not capitalized. *A proper noun* names a specific person, place, or thing. A *common noun* is not specific.

Proper	**Common**
Jeffrey	boy
Houston	city

Directions: Read each sentence. Draw a circle around any proper nouns. Place an X on any common nouns.

1. Jennifer always gets pizza for supper on Fridays.

2. My friend is a nice person.

3. Can you and Joe bake the cake?

4. Mom and Dad are going to the game.

5. Chloe and Kayla Beth are sisters.

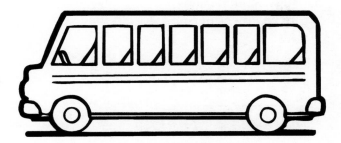

6. The bus took the students to school.

7. Ella gave the teacher an apple.

8. Gage gave the teacher a pencil.

9. Sally saw a huge snake in the tree.

10. The day was Tuesday.

An Interesting Subject

The *subject* of a sentence is who or what it's all about. A noun can be the subject of a sentence.

Directions: Each sentence is missing its subject. Supply a subject by writing a noun on each line.

1. My _____ is broken so I can't use it.

2. My favorite _____ is chocolate pie.

3. Her birthday _____ is next Saturday.

4. The ugly _____ scared me.

5. Bugs, spiders, and _____
   are creepy critters.

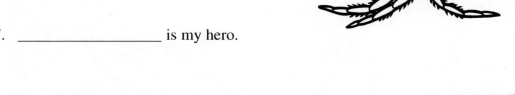

6. _____ is great fun.

7. _____ is my hero.

8. A large _____ was in my mom's car.

Simple Subjects and Simple Predicates

The *simple subject* of a sentence is who or what it's all about. The simple subject is usually a noun. The *simple predicate* of a sentence is what the subject is doing, or it is a word that links the subject to something else.

Dee walks home from school.

The simple subject is *Dee*. The simple predicate is *walks*.

Dee is finally home.

The simple subject is *Dee*. The simple predicate is the word *is*.

Directions: Look at each column. Choose a subject and a predicate. Then use the words in a sentence of your own. You need to write five sentences. If needed, you can add the letters *ed* or *ing* to each predicate.

Subjects	Predicates
cat	swims
tree	walks
boy	ran
Karen	talks
car	is
school	are
teacher	jumps
Ken	yells

1. _____

   _____

2. _____

   _____

3. _____

   _____

4. _____

   _____

5. _____

   _____

Action!

Action verbs are what you do. *Play*, *skip*, and *hop* are all examples of action verbs.

Directions: Find your way from start to finish by coloring only the blocks that have words which can be action verbs.

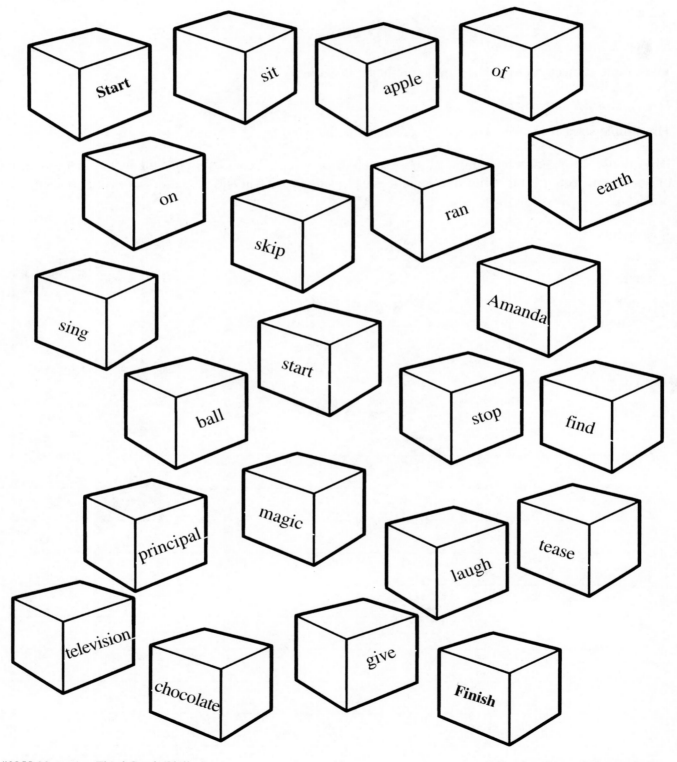

Past or Present

Some verbs tell about things that are happening right now. These are *present tense* verbs.

I cry at sad movies.

Some verbs tell about things that have happened in the past. These are *past tense* verbs.

I cried at the sad movie.

Directions: Each present contains two verbs. Circle the verb that is present tense. Draw a square around the verb that is past tense.

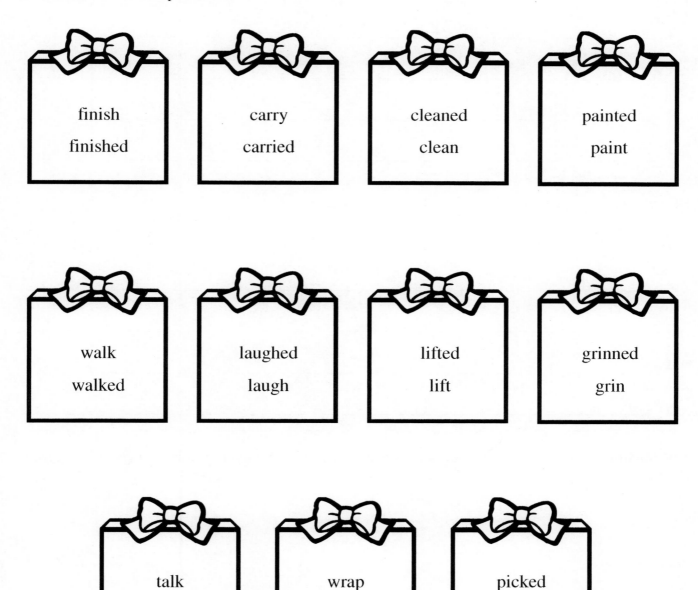

finish
finished

carry
carried

cleaned
clean

painted
paint

walk
walked

laughed
laugh

lifted
lift

grinned
grin

talk
talked

wrap
wrapped

picked
pick

What Did You Do?
When Did You Do It?

Verbs can change tenses. Some verbs are *present tense*, which means the action is happening now, and some are *past tense*, which means the action has happened already.

Directions: List five things you did yesterday. Be sure to use past tense verbs.

1. _____

2. _____

3. _____

4. _____

5. _____

Directions: List five things you like to do. Use present tense verbs.

1. _____

2. _____

3. _____

4. _____

5. _____

Just for fun: In the space below draw a picture of you doing one of your favorite things from the list above.

Add Them In

Directions: Add action verbs to the fairy tale below. Make the story as funny as you would like.
Use present or past tense action verbs in the blanks.

   **The Three Little Pigs . . . Sort of**

Once upon a time there were three little pigs. The pigs all decided to _____ houses. Now, the

first little pig decided to _____ his house out of straw. The second little pig decided to _____

his house out of sticks. And the third little pig _____ to build his house out of bricks.

One day a big, bad wolf came to the house of the first pig (the one who'd built his house out of straw)

and he _____ , "Little pig, if you don't let me in, I'm going to huff and _____ and

_____ your house down." And so . . . he did!

The little pig _____ to his brother's house, but the wolf followed him there. Then he said,

"Little pigs, little pigs, if you don't let me in I'm going to huff and puff and _____ your

house down!" And so . . . he did!

The two little pigs _____ to their third brother's house. His house was made of brick. When

the wolf came and decided to _____ and _____ and blow the house down . . . he

couldn't do it! The house was too strong.

To celebrate, the little pigs decided to _____ a big pot of stew in the fireplace. Little did they

know, the wolf had _____ on the roof and was trying to _____ down the chimney!

The wolf _____ down the chimney and straight into the big pot of boiling stew. He

_____ his tail so badly that he ran straight out the front door, _____ all the way!

And as for the big, bad wolf? Well, let's just _____ he never _____ the three little

pigs again!

Describe It

An *adjective* is a word that describes a noun.

Directions: List two adjectives that can describe each noun.

Example:

apple   <u>red</u>   and   <u>shiny</u>

1. boy   _____ and _____

2. girl   _____ and _____

3. school   _____ and _____

4. dog   _____ and _____

5. home   _____ and _____

6. summer   _____ and _____

7. cars   _____ and _____

8. sports   _____ and _____

9. pizza   _____ and _____

10. flowers   _____ and _____

More with Adjectives

Adjectives describe nouns. They tell *how many*, *which one,* or *what kind* of noun it is.

> Many friends   *how many*
>
> Those friends   *which ones*
>
> Great friends   *what kind*

Directions: Read each sentence. Color each underlined adjective according to the directions below.

> If the adjective tells *how many*, color the word *yellow.*
>
> If the adjective tells *which one*, color the word *blue.*
>
> If the adjective tells *what kind*, color the word *orange.*

1. <u>These</u> grapes are <u>delicious</u>!

2. I like <u>red</u> grapes the best.

3. My <u>favorite</u> grocery store sells the <u>best</u> grapes.

4. <u>Some</u> people only like <u>green</u> grapes.

5. No matter the kind of grapes you like, <u>fresh</u> fruit is always the best.

6. A <u>few</u> grapes are always good to eat each and <u>every</u> day.

7. Whatever you do, don't eat <u>any</u> <u>shriveled</u> grapes!

8. <u>Several</u> friends of mine think I'm crazy to like grapes so much.

9. Maybe they've just never had enough of the <u>delicious</u> fruit.

10. I know I can never get enough of <u>those</u> <u>wonderful</u> grapes.

Telling More about Verbs

Adverbs tell us more about verbs. Adverbs tell *where*, *when*, or *how* about verbs.

We ran quickly.	*how*
Yesterday we ran.	*when*
We ran upstairs.	*where*

Part I

Directions: Look at each question. Use adverbs from the word bank below to describe each event.

soon	tomorrow	today	early	late
inside	outside	slowly	quickly	last
first	next	easily	carefully	now

1. Do you get up _____ or _____ on the weekends?

2. Would you rather be _____ or _____ on a cold day?

3. If you were running in a race, would you rather finish _____ or _____ ?

4. The day after today is _____ .

5. If you are carrying something breakable, you should carry it _____ .

Part II

Directions: Choose five adverbs from the list above and use them in sentences of your own.

6. _____

_____

7. _____

_____

8. _____

_____

9. _____

_____

10. _____

_____

Can You Find Them?

An *adverb* tells more about a verb. An adverb can tell *how, when,* or *where* about the verb.

Directions: Circle the adverb or adverbs in the sentences below.

1. The frightened boy ran quickly.

2. My favorite movie was on television yesterday.

3. Some of my friends want to go now.

4. Adam gladly accepted the award.

5. My best friend is sometimes late.

6. I looked everywhere for the treasure.

7. The snail moved slowly across the sidewalk.

8. I want to go to the mall today.

9. Please go upstairs.

10. We quietly entered the library.

Know When to Capitalize

Some nouns need to be capitalized. These nouns are called *proper nouns*. They name a specific person, place, or thing.

> The *girl* did her homework.
>
> *Casey* did her homework.

Casey names a specific girl and needs to be capitalized.

Directions: Answer each question. Be sure to capitalize any proper nouns that you use.

1. What is your favorite day of the week?_____

2. What is your favorite month? _____

3. In what month were you born? _____

4. What is your last name? _____

5. What is your favorite holiday? _____

6. What is the name of your favorite restaurant? _____

7. What is your favorite sports team? _____

8. In what city do you live? _____

9. In what country do you live?_____

10. What is the name of your favorite movie? _____

Name That Place

Some nouns need to be capitalized. These nouns are called *proper nouns*. They name a specific person, place, or thing. The names of towns, cities, counties, states, etc., are proper nouns and should be capitalized.

Part I

Directions: Read each question and write the answer on the blank provided.

1. In what city is your school located? _____

2. What is the street address for your school?_____

3. In what state do you live? _____

4. What is the capital city of your state? _____

5. In what country do you live? _____

Part II

Directions: Look at each picture below. Write the name of the place where each famous landmark is located.

6.

_____

7.

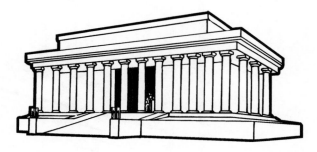

_____

8.

_____

9.

_____

Dear You

One way to stay in touch with someone is to write a letter. When writing a letter, use proper capitalization in the heading, salutation, and closing.

Part I

Directions: Circle the capitalization errors in the letter below.

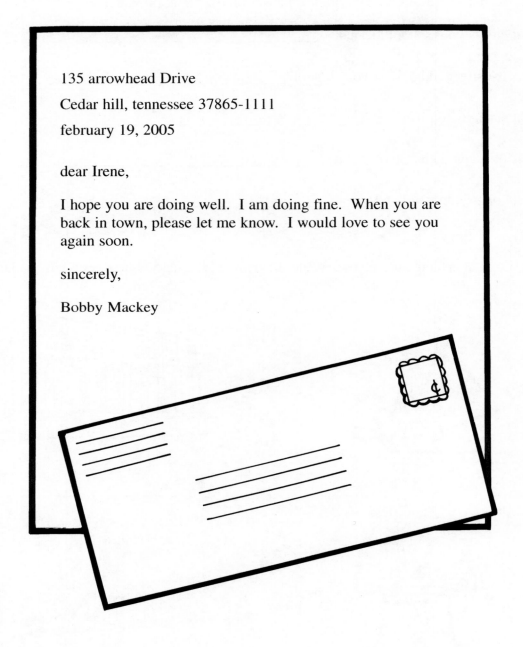

135 arrowhead Drive

Cedar hill, tennessee 37865-1111

february 19, 2005

dear Irene,

I hope you are doing well. I am doing fine. When you are back in town, please let me know. I would love to see you again soon.

sincerely,

Bobby Mackey

Part II

Directions: On the back of this page, write your own letter to someone you'd like to see soon.

Say It with Capitals

When using quotation marks, always capitalize the first letter of the word after the first quotation mark.

Example: Kristen said, "My sister Allison is my best friend."

Directions: Read each quote. Answer with a quote of your own. Be sure to use correct capitalization.

1. Derek said, "Do you want to go out with me?"

   Shea replied, "_____."

2. He asked, "How old are you?"

   She answered, "_____."

3. "Can I help you?" he asked.

   "_____," she responded.

4. Tessa said, "You are a nice brother, Simon."

   Simon replied, "_____."

5. Mark asked, "Could you please keep your room neater?"

   Amanda answered, "_____."

A Boat Load of Trouble

There are capitalization problems on the open seas! See what you can do to help calm the waters.

Directions: Look at the words on the sailboats. Correct any capitalization problems by writing the word correctly in the space provided.

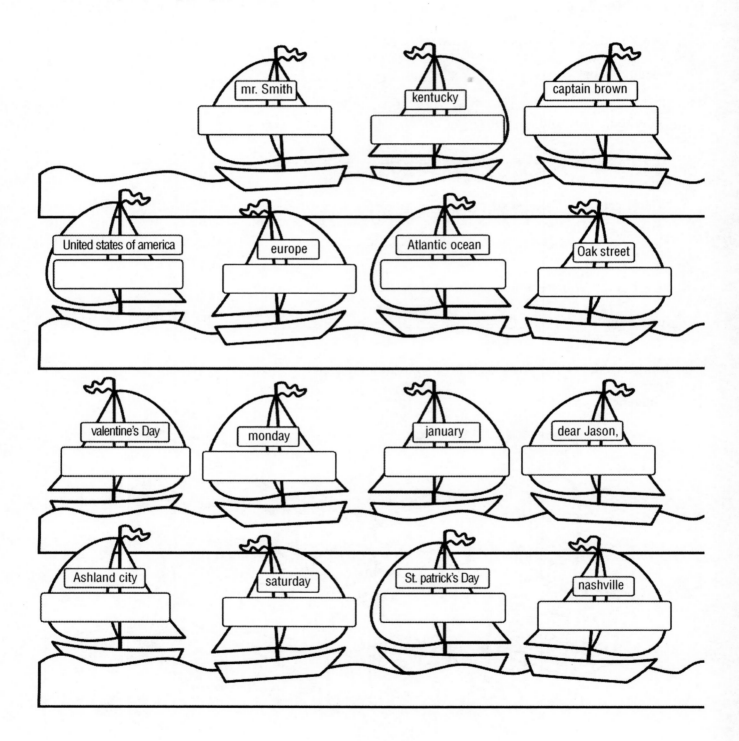

More Than a Dot

A *period* is much more than just a dot. Use a period in initials, abbreviations, and with certain titles before names.

Carla Jean Smith	C. J. Smith
Drive	Dr.
Mister Jones	Mr. Jones

Directions: Look at the spots on the dog below. Each one contains a punctuation mistake. Add periods as needed to correct the problems.

It's All in the End

Always end a statement or a command with a *period*.

Example: Your hair looks icky.

Go wash your hair.

Directions: Finish each statement or command and add the correct ending punctuation.

1. I really like _____

2. Move that _____

3. Get me a _____

4. Chris is a _____

5. Go to the _____

6. We ate _____

7. I hate when _____

8. Take a _____

9. Look at _____

10. Give me _____

The Date and Place

Use a *comma* between the day of the month and the year.

Example: March 3, 1997

Also, use a *comma* between the names of a city and its state.

Example: Louisville, Kentucky

Directions: In each pair, circle the answer that is punctuated correctly.

A	B
1. March 7 1981	March 7, 1981
2. Houston, Texas	Houston Texas,
3. Orlando Florida,	Orlando, Florida
4. November, 7, 2005	November 7, 2005
5. September 12, 2000	September 12 2000
6. Detroit Michigan,	Detroit, Michigan
7. June, 8 1991	June 8, 1991
8. Salt Lake City Utah	Salt Lake City, Utah
9. October 27, 2005	October, 27, 2005
10. Memphis, Tennessee	Memphis Tennessee

Commas in Letters

Commas should be used in the address, greeting, and closing of a letter.

Directions: Look at the letter below. Add commas wherever needed.

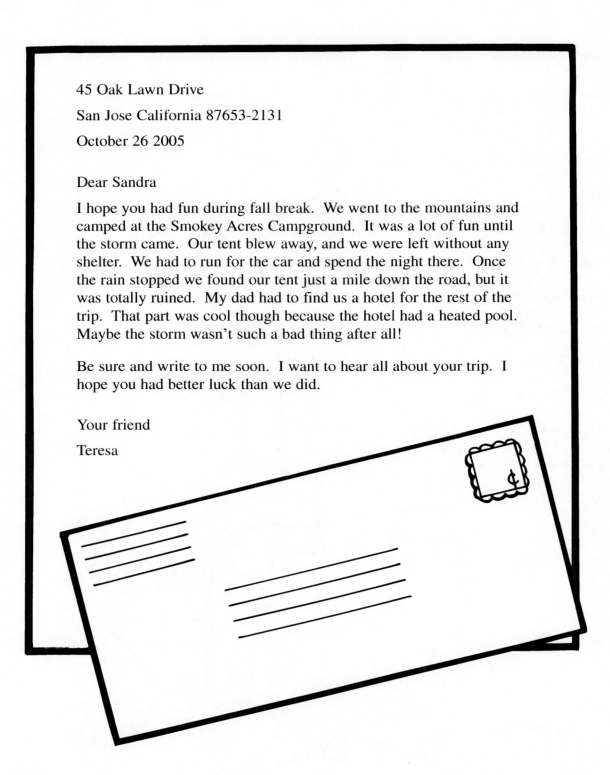

45 Oak Lawn Drive

San Jose California 87653-2131

October 26 2005

Dear Sandra

I hope you had fun during fall break. We went to the mountains and camped at the Smokey Acres Campground. It was a lot of fun until the storm came. Our tent blew away, and we were left without any shelter. We had to run for the car and spend the night there. Once the rain stopped we found our tent just a mile down the road, but it was totally ruined. My dad had to find us a hotel for the rest of the trip. That part was cool though because the hotel had a heated pool. Maybe the storm wasn't such a bad thing after all!

Be sure and write to me soon. I want to hear all about your trip. I hope you had better luck than we did.

Your friend

Teresa

Two into One

An *apostrophe* shows where letters are missing. When two words are made into a new word, that new word is called a *contraction*.

By using an apostrophe, *do not* becomes *don't*. The apostrophe takes the place of the *o* in *not*.

Directions: Draw a line and match each set of words to the correct contraction.

1. does not	a. weren't
2. will not	b. aren't
3. has not	c. hadn't
4. was not	d. doesn't
5. is not	e. Jack's
6. did not	f. hasn't
7. had not	g. wasn't
8. were not	h. isn't
9. are not	i. didn't
10. Jack is	j. won't

What Was It?

An *apostrophe* shows where letters are missing. When two words are made into a new word, that new word is called a *contraction*.

Is not becomes *isn't*. The letter that is missing is the letter *o*, which has been replaced by an apostrophe.

Directions: Read each sentence. Circle the contraction in each sentence. Then, on the line provided, write the two words that make up the contraction.

1. I don't really like him. _____

2. She isn't my friend. _____

3. Olivia can't come to the party. _____

4. We aren't the only ones going. _____

5. He doesn't act like a teacher. _____

6. I haven't found my money yet. _____

7. Michele's going to the movies. _____

8. Natalie won't stop crying. _____ v

9. He's my father's best friend. _____

10. Kimberly and Courtney didn't leave. _____

Playing Genie

An apostrophe can be used with a noun to show possession or ownership. If Kara owns a cat then the apostrophe can help show that it is *Kara's* cat.

Directions: Imagine you are a genie in a bottle and instead of giving out just the standard three wishes, you can grant 10 wishes to anyone you want. Make the following kids' wishes come true by writing and using an apostrophe to give them what they want.

Example: Joe wants a skateboard. *Joe's skateboard*

1. Emily wants some candy.

2. Chien wants a DVD.

3. Tyrese wants a new backpack.

4. Rafael wants a camera.

5. Keysha wants a necklace.

6. Elissa wants a game.

7. Sharon wants a puzzle.

8. Samuel wants some shoes.

9. Aina wants a book.

10. Brody wants a bike.

The Importance of Ownership

An *apostrophe* is used to show possession or ownership. For example, if a woman wants to own a house, an apostrophe can help her do just that.

Example: The *woman's* house

In most cases all you need to do is add an apostrophe and the letter *s*.

Directions: Rewrite each set of words to show ownership.

Example: dog dish   *dog's dish*

1. student lunch _____

2. mother purse _____

3. Bailey toy _____

4. child shoe _____

5. pirate treasure _____

6. bear fur _____

7. tree leaves _____

8. flower petals _____

9. library books _____

10. shark teeth _____

Talk to Me

Quotation marks are used to show that someone is speaking. They come at the beginning and the end of a person's words.

Example: Riley asked, "Do you know the words to this song?"

Quotation marks are not around *Riley asked* because Riley didn't say those words.

Directions: Pretend you have just given your teacher an apple, but when she bit into the delicious treat, she bit into a juicy worm!

What would you say? What would your teacher say to you?

On the lines provided write a short conversation between you and your teacher. Remember to use quotation marks around what was said.

Also, be sure to start on a new line each time you change speakers. This makes your conversation easier to read.

_____

_____

_____

_____

_____

_____

_____

_____

_____

_____

Quotation Marks Mark the Spot

Quotation marks go around a person's exact words. If there is a comma before the quotation, it goes outside the quotation marks. Punctuation at the end of a quotation goes inside the quotation marks.

Example: He said, "I don't want to go."

"But you must be there," she replied.

Directions: Read each quote and add quotation marks wherever they are needed.

1. I can't wait for summer vacation, Ted said.

2. I can't wait either, Addison agreed.

3. Where are you going on vacation? Ted asked.

4. We're going to Hawaii, Addison said.

5. That sounds very nice, Ted replied.

6. Where are you going? Addison asked.

7. Ted replied, Well, it's not exactly Hawaii, but there is water there.

8. Well, where is it? Addison asked again.

9. I'm going to spend my vacation working at my Uncle Bob's carwash, Ted finally told her.

10. I guess you're right. There will be plenty of water, Addison said with a smile.

Not Quite Human

Personification is when a nonliving object is given human characteristics. How can you remember this? Notice the root word of personification is *person*. If a nonliving object is given human characteristics then the writer has used personification.

Example: The sand on the beach ran its grainy fingers along our bare feet.

Directions: Circle the sentences that show examples of personification.

1. I love spaghetti and meatballs.

2. The burnt spaghetti stared at me sadly from my plate.

3. The delicious smell of spaghetti called to me from the kitchen.

4. I don't know which I love more, spaghetti or lasagna.

5. The noodles and red sauce begged for me to eat them.

6. I swallowed them quickly and then hurried to get more.

7. I love spaghetti and my spaghetti loves me.

8. The delicious noodles danced their way to my tummy.

9. If the spaghetti was this good, I knew the dessert would be even better.

10. I heard the chef was serving chocolate-covered spaghetti noodles.

Watch That Twisting Tongue!

Alliteration is the repetition of a consonant sound. Tongue twisters are examples of alliteration.

Example: She sells seashells down by the seashore.

Notice the repetition of the *S* sound.

Directions: Use alliteration to write your own tongue twisters.

1. Write a tongue twister using the sound of the letter *T*.

   _____

   _____

   _____

2. Write a tongue twister using the sound of the letter *S*.

   _____

   _____

   _____

3. Write a tongue twister using the sound of the letter *Z*.

   _____

   _____

   _____

4. Write a tongue twister using the sound of the letter *R*.

   _____

   _____

   _____

Just for fun: In the space below draw an illustration for one of your tongue twisters.

Splat! Bam! Boom!

Onomatopoeia is when a word is used to represent a sound. A bee doesn't really go "buzz," but we use the word *buzz* to represent the sound a bee makes.

Directions: Beside each word write an example of onomatopoeia for the sound each thing makes.

1. A dog wanting attention _____

2. A cat wanting some milk_____

3. A door shutting hard _____

4. A door that needs some oil _____

5. A girl eating a piece of ice_____

6. A balloon being stuck with a nail _____

7. A baby crying _____

8. A librarian warning you to be quiet_____

9. A crowd cheering for a team _____

10. A baby bird wanting a snack_____

This is Like That

A *simile* is a comparison that uses the words *like* or *as* to make the comparison.

Example: My blanket is like a warm, fuzzy bear.

My blanket is as warm as a soft, fuzzy bear.

The blanket is being compared to a warm, fuzzy bear.

Directions: Complete each sentence starter with a simile.

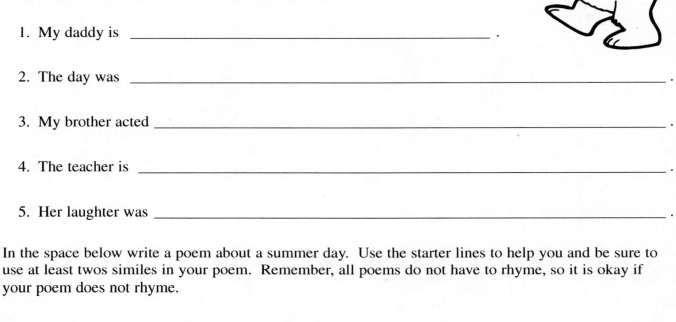

1. My daddy is _____ .

2. The day was _____ .

3. My brother acted _____ .

4. The teacher is _____ .

5. Her laughter was _____ .

In the space below write a poem about a summer day. Use the starter lines to help you and be sure to use at least twos similes in your poem. Remember, all poems do not have to rhyme, so it is okay if your poem does not rhyme.

_____
(Poem Title)

Summer is like a _____

It is as _____as a _____

I like summer because _____

Summer is _____

It Is What It Is

A *metaphor* is a comparison that does not use *like* or *as*.

Example: That boy is a pig.

Is the boy really a pig? Of course not! A metaphor is simply a comparison. Maybe the boy is very messy or maybe he eats a lot.

Directions: Read the poem below. Circle all metaphors in the poem.

Chocolate

Of all the things I love the most,

Some are not that strange.

I love my mother and my father

And even my sister, Lorraine.

But my favorite thing is chocolate.

Chocolate is a dream.

It melts in my mouth.

It is gold for the tongue.

It is always a delicious thing.

I love it because it's easy to get.

Chocolate is definitely heaven.

It's better than caramel or strawberry swirl,

It's certainly better than vanilla.

Chocolate is a cartoon character,

With smiles and laughs for all.

When I eat chocolate, I am so happy;

I feel like I'm ten feet tall!

Bigger and Better

A *hyperbole* is an extreme exaggeration. For example, your big brother might be tall, but if you say that he's so tall he could reach the top of the Empire State Building, then that's an extreme exaggeration.

Part I

Directions: Complete each sentence with a hyperbole of your own.

Example: My cousin is so smart that teachers ask her if the answers are correct or not.

1. My sister is so little _____ .

2. My teacher is so mean _____ .

3. My school is so big _____ .

4. My friends are so nice _____ .

Part II

Directions: Read each statement. If the statement is a hyperbole, write the letter H on the line provided. If it is not a hyperbole, write an X on the line.

_____ 5. Her appetite is so big she can eat every bit of food in the grocery store.

_____ 6. She is the nicest person I know.

_____ 7. This weather is so cold it would make a penguin wear a coat.

_____ 8. My head really, really hurts.

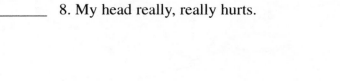

Where Is It?

The *setting* of a story includes all the places where the story happens or takes place. For example, in the story of the "Three Little Pigs," the setting includes all three homes where the pigs live. The straw house, the stick house, and the brick house are all part of the setting.

Directions: Look at each picture. On the line provided, describe each setting.

Example: The setting is a tropical and nearly deserted island.

1.

   _____

2.

   _____

3.

   _____

4.

   _____

5.

   _____

6.

   _____

And the Answer Is...

When you *draw a conclusion* you tell what you think the outcome is going to be. For example, if your class has a field trip to the zoo planned but on the day of the field trip there is a storm, you can probably conclude that the field trip will be cancelled.

Directions: Read each situation and then write what you think the conclusion will be.

1. A little boy brings home a report card with straight A's.

_____

_____

_____

2. A woman sees a dog digging up flowers in her front yard.

_____

_____

_____

3. A little girl leaves her ice cream cone outside in the hot sun.

_____

_____

_____

4. A truck is going down a road. Just ahead there are nails scattered on the road.

_____

_____

_____

5. A mother bird is sitting on her nest. One of her eggs starts to crack.

_____

_____

_____

One Thing Leads to Another

Every *effect* has a *cause*. If you forget to bring your coat to school and it snows while you are at school, you will be cold when it's time to go home.

Example: *Effect:* You are cold.

             Cause: You forgot your coat.

Directions: Match each cause to the correct effect.

1. You have a tooth ache.   A. You make a bad grade.

2. You don't do your homework.   B. They do not grow.

3. You forget to water your plants.   C. You get a lot of presents.

4. You have a birthday party.   D. You get a sunburn.

5. You work outside in the hot sun.   E. You go to the dentist.

Now write a cause and effect for each space below.

6. _____

7. _____

8. _____

9. _____

10. _____

How Would You Behave?

If you are reading a story, you may use *inference* to help you predict how a character will or will not behave. Inference is a guess you make based on what you know.

For example, imagine a very strict teacher who always expects her class to behave. If she has to leave the room for a minute, then comes back to the classroom and the students are throwing paper airplanes and running around the room, how do you think she will react?

If you guessed that she would not be pleased, then you are using inference.

Directions: Read each situation and infer the reaction. Write your answer on the lines provided.

1. A young boy has a piggy bank filled with change. His little sister sneaks in his room and accidentally breaks his bank. The young boy walks into his room and sees change all over the place and his sister looking guilty.

    How do you think he might react? _____

    _____

2. A brother and sister get out of bed on a school day and rush to the window. It is snowing outside! They both received sleds for their birthdays and have been wishing for a snow day to try out their new gifts. Their mother comes into the room and tells them school has been canceled.

    How do you think they might react? _____

    _____

    _____

3. An ice cream truck is coming down the street. A little girl has money and wants to buy some ice cream. On her way to the truck, she sees a sign that says Puppy for Sale. The puppy costs the same amount of money that the little girl has in her hand. She knows her mother and daddy don't want her to have a puppy, but she's always wanted one.

    What do you think she might do? _____

    _____

    _____

    _____

Addition Magician

Directions: Add to find the sum.

1.
$$\begin{array}{r} 5 \\ + 3 \\ \hline \end{array}$$

2.
$$\begin{array}{r} 4 \\ + 4 \\ \hline \end{array}$$

3.
$$\begin{array}{r} 8 \\ + 2 \\ \hline \end{array}$$

4.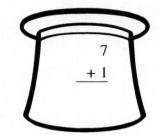
$$\begin{array}{r} 7 \\ + 1 \\ \hline \end{array}$$

5.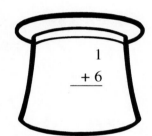
$$\begin{array}{r} 1 \\ + 6 \\ \hline \end{array}$$

6.
$$\begin{array}{r} 2 \\ + 7 \\ \hline \end{array}$$

7.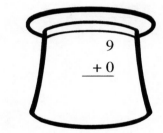
$$\begin{array}{r} 9 \\ + 0 \\ \hline \end{array}$$

8.
$$\begin{array}{r} 4 \\ + 5 \\ \hline \end{array}$$

9.
$$\begin{array}{r} 3 \\ + 3 \\ \hline \end{array}$$

10.
$$\begin{array}{r} 8 \\ + 1 \\ \hline \end{array}$$

11.
$$\begin{array}{r} 2 \\ + 4 \\ \hline \end{array}$$

12.
$$\begin{array}{r} 6 \\ + 4 \\ \hline \end{array}$$

13.
$$\begin{array}{r} 3 \\ + 5 \\ \hline \end{array}$$

14.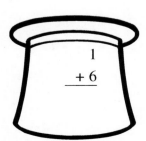
$$\begin{array}{r} 1 \\ + 6 \\ \hline \end{array}$$

15.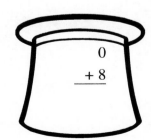
$$\begin{array}{r} 0 \\ + 8 \\ \hline \end{array}$$

Flip Jacks

If someone offered you five pancakes and one pancake would you want them? What if someone offered you one pancake and five pancakes? Would you want them? Which is more?

$$5 + 1 = 6$$
$$1 + 5 = 6$$

Flipping the numbers around in an addition problem does not change the answer.

Directions: Look at each addition problem. Add to find the answer.

1.   5   6   2.   7   8
       + 6   + 5   + 8   + 7

3.   2   8   4.   3   4
       + 8   + 2   + 4   + 3

5.   4   7   6.   9   2
       + 7   + 4   + 2   + 9

7.   3   1   8.   5   3
       + 1   + 3   + 3   + 5

9.   9   8   10.   7   6
       + 8   + 9   + 6   + 7

Do You Know?

Directions: Solve each problem by drawing dots or lines to represent each number. Add to find the sum. Circle the correct answer.

Example: 15 + 11 =

  (A.) 26

  B. 30

  C. 4

  D. 27

1. 18 + 9 =

  A. 23

  B. 26

  C. 9

  D. 27

2. 12 + 12 =

  A 24

  B. 12

  C. 26

  D. 0

3. 6 + 9 =

  A. 17

  B. 15

  C. 3

  D. 16

4. 20 + 8 =

  A. 30

  B. 18

  C. 12

  D. 28

5. 11 + 9 =

  A. 21

  B. 20

  C. 19

  D. 2

Blooming Answers

Math answers are hidden in the flower garden. See if you can find the correct answers hidden inside the flowers.

Directions: Find the missing addend. Write the correct number on the line provided. Then, color only the flowers that have the missing addends.

1. _____ + 9 = 12

6. _____ + 4 = 12

2. 6 + ___ = 10

7. _____ + 5 = 15

3. 18 + ____ = 23

8. 8 + ___ = 17

4. 35 + ____ = 35

9. ___ + 3 = 12

5. 7 + ____ = 7

10. ___ + 5 = 9

Dazzling Double Digits

Directions: Add each problem to find the answer.

1.
$$
\begin{array}{r}
22 \\
+\ 18 \\
\hline
\end{array}
$$

2.
$$
\begin{array}{r}
34 \\
+\ 16 \\
\hline
\end{array}
$$

3.
$$
\begin{array}{r}
62 \\
+\ 39 \\
\hline
\end{array}
$$

4.
$$
\begin{array}{r}
15 \\
+\ 17 \\
\hline
\end{array}
$$

5.
$$
\begin{array}{r}
18 \\
+\ 14 \\
\hline
\end{array}
$$

6.
$$
\begin{array}{r}
21 \\
+\ 19 \\
\hline
\end{array}
$$

7.
$$
\begin{array}{r}
26 \\
+\ 55 \\
\hline
\end{array}
$$

8.
$$
\begin{array}{r}
83 \\
+\ 17 \\
\hline
\end{array}
$$

9.
$$
\begin{array}{r}
61 \\
+\ 19 \\
\hline
\end{array}
$$

10.
$$
\begin{array}{r}
43 \\
+\ 28 \\
\hline
\end{array}
$$

11.
$$
\begin{array}{r}
44 \\
+\ 27 \\
\hline
\end{array}
$$

12.
$$
\begin{array}{r}
66 \\
+\ 24 \\
\hline
\end{array}
$$

13.
$$
\begin{array}{r}
16 \\
+\ 15 \\
\hline
\end{array}
$$

14.
$$
\begin{array}{r}
54 \\
+\ 28 \\
\hline
\end{array}
$$

15.
$$
\begin{array}{r}
23 \\
+\ 19 \\
\hline
\end{array}
$$

16.
$$
\begin{array}{r}
22 \\
+\ 10 \\
\hline
\end{array}
$$

17.
$$
\begin{array}{r}
12 \\
+\ 10 \\
\hline
\end{array}
$$

18.
$$
\begin{array}{r}
18 \\
+\ 13 \\
\hline
\end{array}
$$

19.
$$
\begin{array}{r}
43 \\
+\ 21 \\
\hline
\end{array}
$$

20.
$$
\begin{array}{r}
19 \\
+\ 17 \\
\hline
\end{array}
$$

21.
$$
\begin{array}{r}
50 \\
+\ 33 \\
\hline
\end{array}
$$

Triple the Fun

Part I

Directions: Add the three digit numbers to find the answer.

1.	309 + 208	2.	128 + 222	3.	672 + 109
4.	111 + 119	5.	775 + 127	6.	222 + 219
7.	543 + 318	8.	345 + 425	9.	467 + 314

Part II

Directions: Solve the word problems.

10. Braliegh had 712 pennies. Her friend Serame gave her 157 more pennies. How many pennies did

Braliegh have in all? _____

11. Ella had perfect attendance for 179 days. Gage had perfect attendance for 170 days. All together

how many total days of perfect attendance did they have? _____

12. Anna had 213 baseball cards. Her brother gave her his entire collection of 709 cards. How many

cards did Anna have in her collection then? _____

Going Down!

Part I

Directions: Add 12 columns to find the correct answer.

1.	8 14 + 45	2.	12 + 66 + 21	3.	17 81 + 13

4.	48 17 + 22	5.	52 37 + 6	6.	90 8 + 12

7.	78 10 + 2	8.	43 13 + 51	9.	32 9 + 75

Part II

Directions: Add to find the answers.

10. 7 + 23 + 18 = _____

11. 87 + 10 + 5 = _____

12. 20 + 30 + 40 = _____

13. 15 + 25 + 35 = _____

14. 12 + 24 + 7 = _____

15. 51 + 60 + 3 = _____

16. 33 + 33 + 33 = _____

17. 84 + 2 + 10 = _____

18. 98 + 10 + 2 = _____

19. 62 + 11 + 22 = _____

Putting the Dot in the Right Spot

When you add numbers with decimals be sure to put the decimal in the right spot.

$$
\begin{array}{r}
17.98 \\
+\ 10.11 \\
\hline
28.09
\end{array}
$$

Notice the decimal stays in the same place.

Directions: Add each problem. Be sure to include the decimal.

1. $\begin{array}{r} 11.23 \\ +\ 10.11 \\ \hline \end{array}$

2. $\begin{array}{r} 16.78 \\ +\ 12.12 \\ \hline \end{array}$

3. $\begin{array}{r} 98.12 \\ +\ 1.10 \\ \hline \end{array}$

4. $\begin{array}{r} 20.02 \\ +\ 2.02 \\ \hline \end{array}$

5. $\begin{array}{r} 15.7 \\ +\ 13.9 \\ \hline \end{array}$

6. $\begin{array}{r} 14.2 \\ +\ 2.6 \\ \hline \end{array}$

7. $\begin{array}{r} 72.1 \\ +\ 2.5 \\ \hline \end{array}$

8. $\begin{array}{r} 6.3 \\ +\ 1.8 \\ \hline \end{array}$

9. $\begin{array}{r} 9.88 \\ +\ 1.21 \\ \hline \end{array}$

10. $\begin{array}{r} 8.99 \\ +\ 2.21 \\ \hline \end{array}$

11. $\begin{array}{r} 23.2 \\ +\ 17.3 \\ \hline \end{array}$

12. $\begin{array}{r} 17.89 \\ +\ 16.11 \\ \hline \end{array}$

13. $\begin{array}{r} 7.21 \\ +\ 6.21 \\ \hline \end{array}$

14. $\begin{array}{r} 33.45 \\ +\ 14.44 \\ \hline \end{array}$

15. $\begin{array}{r} 87.01 \\ +\ 12.22 \\ \hline \end{array}$

16. $\begin{array}{r} 22.22 \\ +\ 11.11 \\ \hline \end{array}$

17. $\begin{array}{r} 77.87 \\ +\ 18.78 \\ \hline \end{array}$

18. $\begin{array}{r} 64.46 \\ +\ 46.64 \\ \hline \end{array}$

Just Warming Up

Part I

Directions: Subtract to find the answer.

1.
$\begin{array}{r} 9 \\ -6 \\ \hline \end{array}$

2.
$\begin{array}{r} 7 \\ -2 \\ \hline \end{array}$

3.
$\begin{array}{r} 8 \\ -1 \\ \hline \end{array}$

4.
$\begin{array}{r} 3 \\ -2 \\ \hline \end{array}$

5.
$\begin{array}{r} 6 \\ -5 \\ \hline \end{array}$

6.
$\begin{array}{r} 4 \\ -2 \\ \hline \end{array}$

7.
$\begin{array}{r} 9 \\ -7 \\ \hline \end{array}$

8.
$\begin{array}{r} 1 \\ -1 \\ \hline \end{array}$

9.
$\begin{array}{r} 5 \\ -1 \\ \hline \end{array}$

10.
$\begin{array}{r} 7 \\ -4 \\ \hline \end{array}$

11.
$\begin{array}{r} 8 \\ -2 \\ \hline \end{array}$

12.
$\begin{array}{r} 6 \\ -3 \\ \hline \end{array}$

Part II

Directions: Subtract to find the answer.

13. $8 - 5 =$ _____

14. $6 - 4 =$ _____

15. $7 - 3 =$ _____

16. $4 - 1 =$ _____

17. $5 - 2 =$ _____

18. $3 - 3 =$ _____

19. $9 - 6 =$ _____

20. $8 - 3 =$ _____

Subtraction Reaction

Directions: Subtract to find each answer. If the answer is greater than 50, draw a smiley face beside the answer. If the answer is less than 50, draw a frowning face beside the answer.

1. 88
   − 14
   ☐

2. 21
   − 10
   ☐

3. 76
   − 19
   ☐

4. 65
   − 18
   ☐

5. 77
   − 12
   ☐

6. 40
   − 33
   ☐

7. 86
   − 17
   ☐

8. 51
   − 23
   ☐

9. 99
   − 33
   ☐

10. 75
    − 25
    ☐

11. 26
    − 13
    ☐

12. 17
    − 16
    ☐

13. 50
    − 48
    ☐

14. 39
    − 29
    ☐

15. 87
    − 77
    ☐

In the space below, create and answer four subtraction problems of your own. Remember to draw a smiley or frowning face beside your answer.

16. _____
   + _____
   ☐

17. _____
   + _____
   ☐

18. _____
   + _____
   ☐

19. _____
   + _____
   ☐

Take Away

Part I

Directions: Complete each equation

1. $35 - \underline{\hspace{1cm}} = 7$

2. $18 - \underline{\hspace{1cm}} = 9$

3. $\underline{\hspace{1cm}} - 2 = 18$

4. $76 - \underline{\hspace{1cm}} = 33$

5. $89 - \underline{\hspace{1cm}} = 32$

6. $900 - \underline{\hspace{1cm}} = 400$

7. $\underline{\hspace{1cm}} - 356 = 0$

8. $49 - \underline{\hspace{1cm}} = 7$

9. $100 - \underline{\hspace{1cm}} = 50$

10. $\underline{\hspace{1cm}} - 6 = 6$

Part II

Directions: Subtract to find the answer.

11. $\begin{array}{r} 55 \\ -\ 22 \\ \hline \end{array}$

12. $\begin{array}{r} 98 \\ -\ 43 \\ \hline \end{array}$

13. $\begin{array}{r} 43 \\ -\ 12 \\ \hline \end{array}$

14. $\begin{array}{r} 76 \\ -\ 45 \\ \hline \end{array}$

15. $\begin{array}{r} 78 \\ -\ 20 \\ \hline \end{array}$

16. $\begin{array}{r} 44 \\ -\ 17 \\ \hline \end{array}$

17. $\begin{array}{r} 85 \\ -\ 40 \\ \hline \end{array}$

18. $\begin{array}{r} 30 \\ -\ 15 \\ \hline \end{array}$

19. $\begin{array}{r} 21 \\ -\ 11 \\ \hline \end{array}$

20. $\begin{array}{r} 66 \\ -\ 33 \\ \hline \end{array}$

21. $\begin{array}{r} 12 \\ -\ 2 \\ \hline \end{array}$

22. $\begin{array}{r} 90 \\ -\ 45 \\ \hline \end{array}$

Right on Target

Directions: Solve each subtraction problem to hit the center of the target.

1.   754
    − 135

2.   888
    − 777

3.   721
    − 432

4.   312
    − 289

5.   211
    − 101

6.   621
    − 403

7.   110
    − 100

8.   389
    − 299

9.   498
    − 150

10.   923
    − 554

11.   117
    − 117

12.   827
    − 236

13.   909
    − 181

14.   131
    − 121

15.   620
    − 559

Practice, Practice, Practice

Directions: Subtract to find the correct answer.

1. 431
   − 219
   _____

2. 786
   − 354
   _____

3. 871
   − 444
   _____

4. 761
   − 321
   _____

5. 647
   − 456
   _____

6. 321
   − 201
   _____

7. 987
   − 625
   _____

8. 651
   − 412
   _____

9. 777
   − 563
   _____

10. 679
    − 324
    _____

11. 411
    − 346
    _____

12. 983
    − 890
    _____

13. 781
    − 708
    _____

14. 677
    − 667
    _____

15. 156
    − 121
    _____

16. 475
    − 129
    _____

17. 390
    − 187
    _____

18. 290
    − 117
    _____

19. 601
    − 501
    _____

20. 290
    − 190
    _____

21. 195
    − 183
    _____

22. 486
    − 412
    _____

23. 764
    − 378
    _____

24. 905
    − 598
    _____

Word Problem Subtraction

Directions: Solve each word problem. Be sure to show your work.

1. Mrs. Willis has 33 students in her homeroom class. Her afternoon class has 18 students. How many more students does she have in the morning than in the afternoon? _____

2. The annual Turtle Derby is next Saturday. There are 52 turtles entered in the race. The committee hoped to have 78 turtles in the race. How many more turtles do they need to reach their goal?
_____

3. Mr. Mackey runs the local candy shop. Last year he sold 700 candy bars in his shop. This year he has already sold 950 candy bars. How many more candy bars has he sold this year than last year? _____

4. Sophie and her brother Jake opened a lemonade stand. Sophie sold 57 glasses of lemonade by the end of the day. Jake turned his lemonade into lemonade popsicles. By the end of the day Jake had sold 88 lemonade popsicles. How many more lemonade products did Jake sell than Sophie?

_____

5. Sammy Squirrel has been putting away acorns all winter long. He has 967 acorns for the long, cold winter. Sammy's cousin, Charlie Chipmunk, has only 200 acorns tucked away in his house. How many more acorns does Sammy have for the winter months than Charlie? _____

In the space below write a subtraction word problem of your own. Be sure to solve your problem when you are finished.

_____

_____

_____

_____

How Much?

Directions: Solve each problem. Use your answers to solve the riddle below by matching each letter to its answer.

1. $84.67
   − 44.12
   (R)

2. $22.18
   − 10.09
   (O)

3. $33.87
   − 12.22
   (R)

4. $88.02
   − 70.01
   (G)

5. $67.07
   − 23.68
   (G)

6. $87.66
   − 40.22
   (T)

7. $14.07
   − 12.07
   (O)

8. $21.22
   − 15.02
   (E)

9. $39.19
   − 30.09
   (N)

10. $97.11
    − 17.11
    (W)

11. $76.43
    − 16.23
    (E)

12. $55.55
    − 45.35
    (N)

13. $91.60
    − 90.12
    (S)

14. $19.19
    − 12.07
    (I)

Where will you never find money?

___   ___   ___   ___   ___   ___   ___
$43.39 $40.55 $2.00 $80.00 $7.12 $10.20 $18.01

___   ___   ___   ___   ___   ___   ___
$12.09 $9.10 $47.44 $21.65 $6.20 $60.20 $1.48   !

Adding and Multiplying
Go Hand in Hand

Directions: Complete each pair of number sentences.

1. 4 + 4 + 4 + 4 =   4 x 4 =

2. 5 + 5 + 5 + 5 + 5 =   5 x 5 =

3. 6 + 6 + 6 =   6 x 3 =

4. 2 + 2 + 2 + 2 + 2 + 2 =   2 x 6 =

5. 8 + 8 =   8 x 2 =

6. 1 + 1 + 1 + 1 + 1 + 1 + 1 =   1 x 7 =

7. 3 + 3 + 3 =   3 x 3 =

8. 7 + 7 + 7 + 7 =   7 x 4 =

3...2...1...Blast Off!

Directions: Multiply to find the answer.

1. 3 x 1 = _____

2. 2 x 2 = _____

3. 2 x 3 = _____

4. 1 x 9 = _____

5. 3 x 7 = _____

6. 2 x 8 = _____

7. 1 x 6 = _____

8. 2 x 5 = _____

9. 3 x 6 = _____

10. 3 x 8 = _____

More with Multiplication

Directions: Answer these multiplication problems with 4, 5, and 6 as factors.

1. 4 x 4 = _____

2. 5 x 5 = _____

3. 6 x 6 = _____

4. 4 x 0 = _____

5. 5 x 0 = _____

6. 6 x 0 = _____

7. 4 x 3 = _____

8. 5 x 3 = _____

9. 6 x 3 = _____

10. 4 x 7 = _____

11. 5 x 7 = _____

12. 6 x 7 = _____

13. 4 x 10 = _____

14. 5 x 10 = _____

15. 6 x 10 = _____

16. 4 x 8 = _____

17. 5 x 8 = _____

18. 6 x 8 = _____

19. 4 x 2 = _____

20. 5 x 2 = _____

21. 6 x 2 = _____

22. 4 x 5 = _____

23. 5 x 5 = _____

24. 6 x 5 = _____

25. 4 x 9 = _____

26. 5 x 9 = _____

27. 6 x 9 = _____

28. 4 x 12 = _____

29. 5 x 12 = _____

30. 6 x 12 = _____

Learning Your Times: 7, 8, and 9

Directions: Multiply to find each product.

1.   7
       x 1

2.   8
       x 7

3.   7
       x 3

4.   9
       x 6

5.   9
       x 0

6.   7
       x 6

7.   8
       x 3

8.   7
       x 2

9.   8
       x 9

10.   7
       x 4

11.   9
       x 2

12.   7
       x 8

13.   9
       x 3

14.   7
       x 5

15.   8
       x 6

16.   9
       x 10

17.   8
       x 12

18.   9
       x 11

19.   8
       x 8

20.   7
       x 7

Going to the Dogs

Directions: Solve each multiplication problem. If the product is greater than 70, color the dog nearest the problem. If the product is less than 70, then draw an X on the dog nearest the problem.

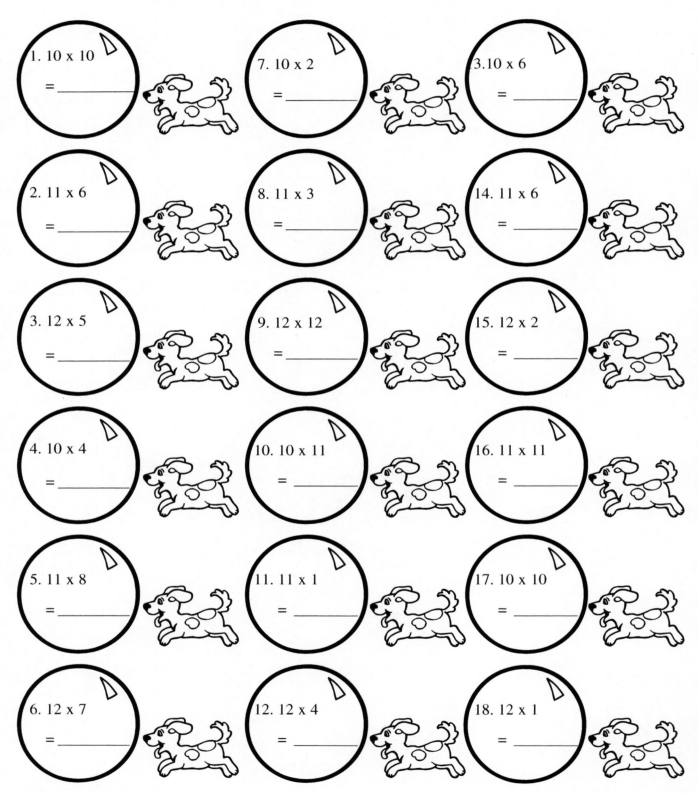

Multiplication Trail

Directions: Follow the path from home to school to get you through the multiplication review.

14. 4 x 4 =

15. 9 x 9 =

13. 10 x 3 =

12. 2 x 9 =

11. 3 x 7 =

10. 11 x 12 =

8. 5 x 9 =

9. 6 x 12 =

7. 1 x 0 =

6. 7 x 9 =

5. 9 x 3 =

4. 8 x 2 =

1. 2 x 2 =

2. 12 x 10 =

3. 4 x 7 =

Beginning to Understand Division

When you divide things, you try to put them into equal groups. If you have 6 blocks, you can divide them into 2 groups of 3 or 3 groups of 2.

However, some numbers do not divide evenly. If you have 7 blocks you can divide them into 2 groups of 3 or 3 groups of 2 but in both cases you would have 1 block left over. This extra number in division is called a *remainder*.

Directions: Divide each set into two equal groups by drawing a box around each group. If there is a remainder, circle the remainder

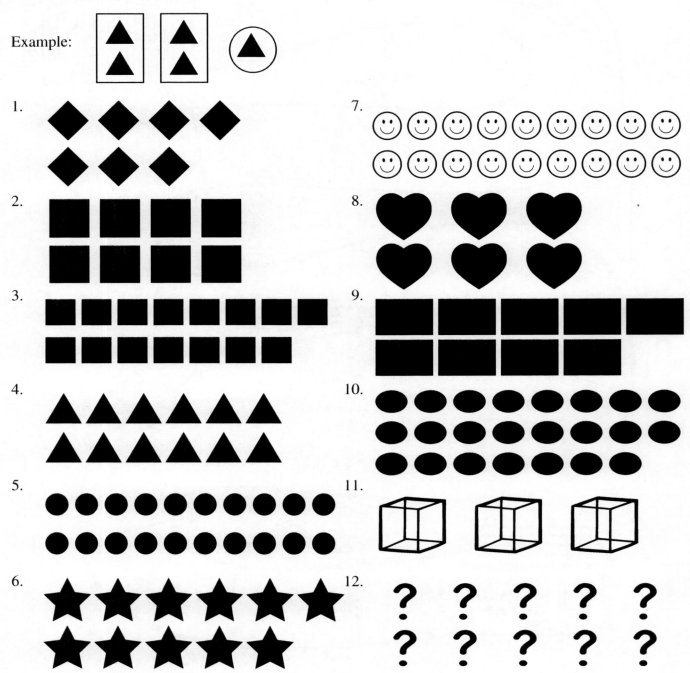

Dividing with 2's and 3's

Part I

Directions: Divide by 2 to find the answer.

1. $18 \div 2 =$ _____

2. $10 \div 2 =$ _____

3. $24 \div 2 =$ _____

4. $8 \div 2 =$ _____

5. $16 \div 2 =$ _____

6. $20 \div 2 =$ _____

7. $6 \div 2 =$ _____

8. $14 \div 2 =$ _____

9. $22 \div 2 =$ _____

Part II

Directions: Divide by 3 to find the answer.

10. $9 \div 3 =$ _____

11. $12 \div 3 =$ _____

12. $24 \div 3 =$ _____

13. $18 \div 3 =$ _____

14. $21 \div 3 =$ _____

15. $15 \div 3 =$ _____

16. $6 \div 3 =$ _____

17. $27 \div 3 =$ _____

18. $33 \div 3 =$ _____

Part III

Directions: Write the missing number.

19. $24 \div$ _____ $= 12$

20. $30 \div$ _____ $= 10$

21. $36 \div$ _____ $= 12$

22. $12 \div$ _____ $= 6$

23. $22 \div$ _____ $= 11$

24. $8 \div$ _____ $= 4$

4, 5, and 6...Learn Division Quack

Directions: Look at each division problem. If the problem is correct, color the duck. If the problem is not correct, draw an X on the duck.

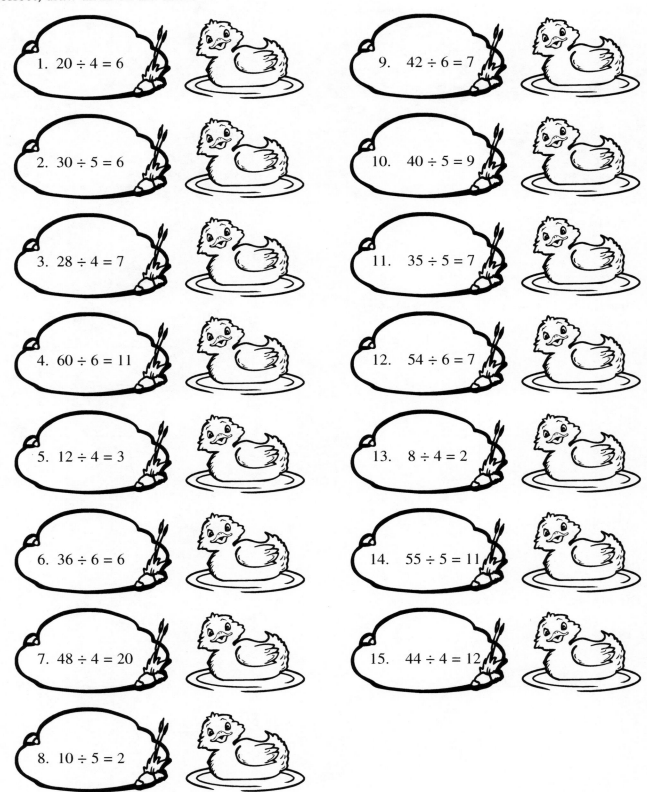

1. $20 \div 4 = 6$

2. $30 \div 5 = 6$

3. $28 \div 4 = 7$

4. $60 \div 6 = 11$

5. $12 \div 4 = 3$

6. $36 \div 6 = 6$

7. $48 \div 4 = 20$

8. $10 \div 5 = 2$

9. $42 \div 6 = 7$

10. $40 \div 5 = 9$

11. $35 \div 5 = 7$

12. $54 \div 6 = 7$

13. $8 \div 4 = 2$

14. $55 \div 5 = 11$

15. $44 \div 4 = 12$

7, 8, and 9 – Solve the Riddle Every Time

Directions: Solve each division problem to find the hidden sentence below.

1. $21 \div 7 =$ _____ O

2. $16 \div 8 =$ _____ R

3. $81 \div 9 =$ _____ Y

4. $40 \div 8 =$ _____ U

5. $56 \div 8 =$ _____ M

6. $108 \div 9 =$ _____ S

7. $7 \div 7 =$ _____ A

8. $32 \div 8 =$ _____ A

9. $99 \div 9 =$ _____ T

10. $42 \div 7 =$ _____ E

11. $72 \div 9 =$ _____ R

___ ___ ___   ___ ___ ___   ___ ___ ___ ___ ___!
9   3   5   1   2   6   12   7   4   8   11

Double Digits...10, 11, and 12

Directions: Solve each division problem. Circle the correct answer.

1. $36 \div 12 =$

    a. 13

    b. 3

    c. 2

2. $22 \div 11 =$

    a. 2

    b. 10

    c. 11

3. $100 \div 10 =$

    a. 9

    b. 20

    c. 10

4. $121 \div 11 =$

    a. 12

    b. 10

    c. 11

5. $48 \div 12 =$

    a. 8

    b. 6

    c. 4

6. $33 \div 11 =$

    a. 11

    b. 3

    c. 6

7. $60 \div 12 =$

    a. 5

    b. 8

    c. 3

8. $70 \div 10 =$

    a. 10

    b. 11

    c. 7

9. $55 \div 11 =$

    a. 11

    b. 5

    c. 1

10. $24 \div 12 =$

    a. 12

    b. 4

    c. 2

11. $20 \div 10 =$

    a. 2

    b. 10

    c. 20

12. $110 \div 11 =$

    a. 11

    b. 12

    c. 10

13. $96 \div 12 =$

    a. 12

    b. 9

    c. 8

14. $77 \div 11 =$

    a. 11

    b. 7

    c. 10

Dividing and Multiplying Go Together

Directions: Complete each set of related problems.

1. 27 ÷ 3 = _____   3 x 9 = _____

2. 12 ÷ 4 = _____   4 x 3 = _____

3. 18 ÷ 6 = _____   6 x 3 = _____

4. 10 ÷ 2 = _____   2 x 5 = _____

5. 88 ÷ 11 = _____   11 x 8 = _____

6. 45 ÷ 9 = _____   9 x 5 = _____

7. 7 ÷ 1 = _____   1 x 7 = _____

8. 28 ÷ 4 = _____   4 x 7 = _____

9. 36 ÷ 3 = _____   3 x 12 = _____

10. 60 ÷ 10 = _____   0 x 6 = _____

11. 44 ÷ 4 = _____   4 x 11 = _____

12. 24 ÷ 6 = _____   6 x 4 = _____

13. 50 ÷ 5 = _____   5 x 10 = _____

14. 56 ÷ 8 = _____   8 x 7 = _____

15. 14 ÷ 2 = _____   2 x 7 = _____

16. 48 ÷ 4 = _____   4 x 12 = _____

Which One's Right?

Directions: Divide each problem. Be sure to show your work. Then, circle the correct answer

1.

    a. 140

    b. 17 $2\overline{)140}$

    c. 70

    d. 40

2.

    a. 16

    b. 60 $3\overline{)180}$

    c. 90

    d. 18

3.

    a. 7

    b. 6 $4\overline{)28}$

    c. 4

    d. 12

4.

    a. 10

    b. 12 $11\overline{)121}$

    c. 11

    d. 15

5.

    a. 4

    b. 14 $9\overline{)360}$

    c. 36

    d. 40

6.

    a. 111

    b. 22 $2\overline{)222}$

    c. 12

    d. 120

7.

    a. 70

    b. 17 $7\overline{)490}$

    c. 60

    d. 80

8.

    a. 170

    b. 56 $8\overline{)560}$

    c. 70

    d. 80

Quick Division

Part I

Directions: Find the answer to each division problem.

1. $50 \div 10 =$ _____

2. $60 \div 6 =$ _____

3. $20 \div 2 =$ _____

4. $55 \div 11 =$ _____

5. $40 \div 2 =$ _____

6. $80 \div 4 =$ _____

7. $90 \div 9 =$ _____

8. $100 \div 10 =$ _____

9. $10 \div 2 =$ _____

10. $30 \div 10 =$ _____

11. $30 \div 3 =$ _____

12. $88 \div 11 =$ _____

Part II

Directions Complete each equation.

13. _____ $\div 10 = 70$

14. $100 \div$ _____ $= 10$

15. $50 \div$ _____ $= 5$

16. _____ $\div 10 = 8$

17. $55 \div$ _____ $= 11$

18. $20 \div$ _____ $= 10$

19. _____ $\div 10 = 4$

20. $30 \div$ _____ $= 3$

Patterns in Division

Directions: You can do long division problems quickly if you understand the pattern. Find the pattern for each set of division problems. Then divide to find the answer

1. $2\overline{)4}$ $2\overline{)40}$ $2\overline{)400}$ $2\overline{)4,000}$

2. $2\overline{)6}$ $2\overline{)60}$ $2\overline{)600}$ $2\overline{)6,000}$

3. $7\overline{)28}$ $7\overline{)280}$ $7\overline{)2,800}$ $7\overline{)28,000}$

4. $1\overline{)6}$ $1\overline{)60}$ $1\overline{)600}$ $1\overline{)6,000}$

5. $4\overline{)20}$ $4\overline{)200}$ $4\overline{)2,000}$ $4\overline{)20,000}$

6. $3\overline{)9}$ $3\overline{)90}$ $3\overline{)900}$ $3\overline{)9,000}$

7. $5\overline{)5}$ $5\overline{)50}$ $5\overline{)500}$ $5\overline{)5,000}$

8. $8\overline{)32}$ $8\overline{)320}$ $8\overline{)3,200}$ $8\overline{)32,000}$

9. $6\overline{)12}$ $6\overline{)120}$ $6\overline{)1,200}$ $6\overline{)12,000}$

10. $9\overline{)18}$ $9\overline{)180}$ $9\overline{)1,800}$ $9\overline{)18,000}$

And Some Left Over

Sometimes when you divide, the problem doesn't work out evenly. When this happens you have a remainder.

Example:
$$6\overline{)44} \quad \begin{array}{r} 7 \ \ R2 \\ \hline 44 \\ 42 \\ \hline 2 \end{array}$$

Directions: Divide each problem. Be sure to show your work.

1. $2\overline{)73}$ 2. $4\overline{)75}$ 3. $8\overline{)97}$ 4. $9\overline{)98}$

5. $7\overline{)93}$ 6. $6\overline{)62}$ 7. $4\overline{)79}$ 8. $2\overline{)57}$

9. $2\overline{)29}$ 10. $4\overline{)15}$ 11. $3\overline{)82}$ 12. $6\overline{)73}$

13. $3\overline{)55}$ 14. $6\overline{)15}$ 15. $2\overline{)49}$ 16. $7\overline{)17}$

17. $3\overline{)38}$ 18. $5\overline{)74}$ 19. $8\overline{)97}$ 20. $9\overline{)63}$

Directions: Solve the following word problem.

13. Tucker has 89 pieces of bubble gum. He divides them between his brother Preston and himself. How may pieces will each boy get if the pieces are divided equally? Will there be any pieces remaining? _____

A Part of the Whole

A *fraction* is a part of a whole. If you had a pizza for dinner and the pizza was cut into 8 equal slices, each slice would represent $\frac{1}{8}$ of the pizza. It would take 8 $\frac{1}{8}$'s to make a whole pizza.

Directions: Draw a line and match the correct picture with the fraction that represents the picture.

1.   a. $\frac{1}{4}$

2.   b. $\frac{4}{8}$

3.   c. $\frac{2}{3}$

4.   d. $\frac{1}{3}$

5.   e. $\frac{1}{2}$

6.   f. $\frac{3}{8}$

Directions: Read each fraction given and draw a picture to show that amount. **Hint:** It's easier to draw fractions using geometric shapes like circles, squares, and rectangles.

7. $\frac{1}{2}$ 8. $\frac{2}{5}$

9. $\frac{1}{6}$ 10. $\frac{4}{10}$

A Part of the Group

A fraction can be used to name a part of a group. For example, pretend your friends are planning a trip to the movies. Of the five friends, three want to see a comedy but the other two want to go to a scary movie. This decision can be shown using fractions.

 $\frac{3}{5}$ of your friends want to go to a comedy.

$\frac{2}{5}$ of your friends want to go to a scary movie.

Directions: Look at each group and write a fraction for the answer.

Example: How many of the stars have stripes?    $\frac{3}{5}$ have stripes.

1. What fraction of the circles have polka dots?   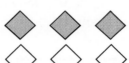   _____

2. What fraction of the diamonds are shaded in?   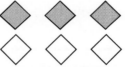   _____

3. What fraction of the triangles are shaded in?   _____

4. What fraction ladybugs have dots?      _____

5. What fraction of the squares have stripes?   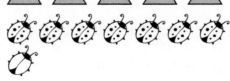   _____

6. What fraction of the ants are shaded in?      _____

7. What fraction of the circles have smiley faces?   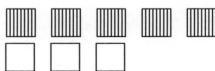   _____

8. What fraction of the squares are shaded in?      _____

Cooking with Fractions

Fractions are used in real life all the time. One way fractions are used is in recipes. If you bake cookies, cakes, or pies, you are definitely going to use fractions.

Example: Something Extra Ice Cream

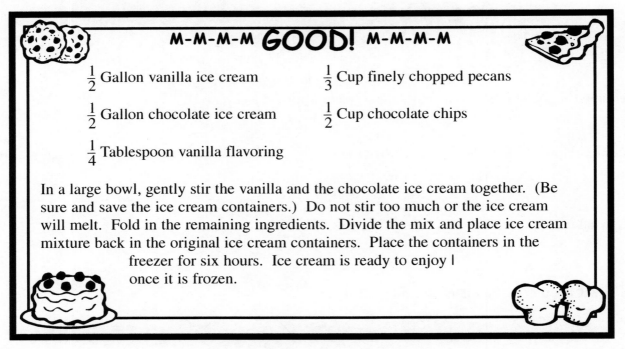

M-M-M-M **GOOD!** M-M-M-M

$\frac{1}{2}$ Gallon vanilla ice cream $\frac{1}{3}$ Cup finely chopped pecans

$\frac{1}{2}$ Gallon chocolate ice cream $\frac{1}{2}$ Cup chocolate chips

$\frac{1}{4}$ Tablespoon vanilla flavoring

In a large bowl, gently stir the vanilla and the chocolate ice cream together. (Be sure and save the ice cream containers.) Do not stir too much or the ice cream will melt. Fold in the remaining ingredients. Divide the mix and place ice cream mixture back in the original ice cream containers. Place the containers in the freezer for six hours. Ice cream is ready to enjoy I once it is frozen.

Directions: Imagine you are a famous chef and you are writing a cookbook. Below are several dishes that will be in your cookbook. What's the catch? You have to write the recipe. Be sure to use at least four fractions in each of your creations. Also, don't forget the cooking directions! Bon appetit!

M-M-M-M **GOOD!** M-M-M-M

1. World's Best Chocolate Cake

M-M-M-M **GOOD!** M-M-M-M

2. Meat Lover's Perfect Pizza

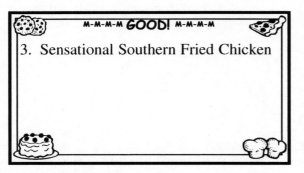

M-M-M-M **GOOD!** M-M-M-M

3. Sensational Southern Fried Chicken

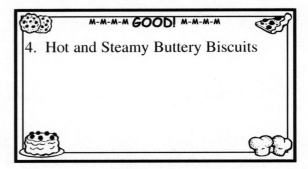

M-M-M-M **GOOD!** M-M-M-M

4. Hot and Steamy Buttery Biscuits

Adding and Subtracting Fractions

When the bottom numbers of fractions are the same, those fractions can be added or subtracted.

$$\frac{1}{4} + \frac{2}{4} = \frac{3}{4} \qquad \text{and} \qquad \frac{3}{4} - \frac{1}{4} = \frac{2}{4}$$

Notice that the bottom number (the denominator) stays the same—only the top number (the numerator) changes.

Part I

Directions: Add the following fractions.

1. $\frac{2}{5} + \frac{3}{5} =$ _____

2. $\frac{1}{8} + \frac{4}{8} =$ _____

3. $\frac{1}{3} + \frac{1}{3} =$ _____

4. $\frac{2}{6} + \frac{3}{6} =$ _____

5. $\frac{1}{4} + \frac{3}{4} =$ _____

6. $\frac{4}{10} + \frac{3}{10} =$ _____

Part II

Directions: Subtract the following fractions.

7. $\frac{4}{8} - \frac{1}{8} =$ _____

8. $\frac{5}{6} - \frac{2}{6} =$ _____

9. $\frac{7}{10} - \frac{3}{10} =$ _____

10. $\frac{3}{4} - \frac{2}{4} =$ _____

11. $\frac{3}{3} - \frac{2}{3} =$ _____

12. $\frac{8}{9} - \frac{6}{9} =$ _____

Part III

Directions: Solve each problem and draw a picture to represent the answer.

13. $\frac{2}{3} + \frac{1}{3} =$ _____

14. $\frac{2}{6} - \frac{1}{6} =$ _____

More Adding and Subtracting with Fractions

Directions: Underline all of the subtraction problems with a blue crayon. Underline all of the addition problems with a red crayon. Then, add or subtract the fractions to find the answers.

1. $\frac{1}{2} - \frac{1}{2} =$ _____

2. $\frac{3}{4} + \frac{1}{4} =$ _____

3. $\frac{4}{8} + \frac{2}{8} =$ _____

4. $\frac{7}{8} - \frac{4}{8} =$ _____

5. $\frac{4}{7} - \frac{2}{7} =$ _____

6. $\frac{4}{5} + \frac{1}{5} =$ _____

7. $\frac{2}{3} + \frac{1}{3} =$ _____

8. $\frac{8}{12} - \frac{3}{12} =$ _____

9. $\frac{4}{6} + \frac{1}{6} =$ _____

10. $\frac{4}{8} + \frac{2}{8} =$ _____

11. $\frac{4}{8} - \frac{2}{8} =$ _____

12. $\frac{2}{6} + \frac{2}{6} =$ _____

13. $\frac{2}{3} - \frac{1}{3} =$ _____

14. $\frac{7}{8} - \frac{1}{8} =$ _____

15. $\frac{3}{10} + \frac{7}{10} =$ _____

16. $\frac{5}{12} + \frac{4}{12} =$ _____

17. $\frac{8}{9} - \frac{2}{9} =$ _____

18. $\frac{5}{6} - \frac{3}{6} =$ _____

Beginning Probability with Fractions

The probability of something happening is the same thing as the chance of something happening. A probability can be written as a fraction.

If you have a quarter and you flip the quarter in the air, the probability or chance that the quarter will land on "heads" is 1 in 2 or $\frac{1}{2}$.

Directions: Read each problem. Write the probability as a fraction.

1. Marcus has a penny in his pocket. When he pulls out the penny to put it in his piggy bank, he drops the penny. What is the probability that the penny will land with the Lincoln side facing up?

   _____

2. A red-haired girl and a blonde-haired girl walk into a store. What is the probability that the red-haired girl will leave the store first? _____

3. Maggie and Hannah are at dance class. Miss Jennifer, the teacher, asks one of the girls to lead the dance line. What is the probability Riley will lead the line? _____

4. Two prizes are placed in a prize box. One is a candy bar. The other is a sucker. What is the probability of someone pulling the candy bar out of the prize box? _____

5. Kelly's parents are trying to decide where to go on vacation. Her mother wants to go to Florida. Her father wants to go to New Mexico. What is the probability they will go to New Mexico?

   _____

Probable Probability

Remember that probability can be written as a fraction. Suppose you have three friends, Jack, Sarah, and Candy, who usually call you. The phone rings early on Saturday morning, and your mother answers it. She tells you the phone is for you and that it is one of your friends. What is the probability of answering the phone and finding out that it is Jack who has called you?

The probability of Jack being on the line is 1 in 3 or $\frac{1}{3}$.

Directions: Read each problem. Circle the correct answer.

1. Four balls are placed in a box. One is red, one is green, one is yellow, and one is blue. What is the probability of pulling a red ball from the box?

   a. $\frac{1}{3}$

   b. $\frac{2}{4}$

   c. $\frac{1}{4}$

2. Two kittens are hiding under a chair. One kitten is a fluffy girl kitten. The other kitten is a fluffy boy kitten. What is the probability of the boy kitten coming out from under the chair first?

   a. $\frac{1}{3}$

   b. $\frac{1}{2}$

   c. $\frac{2}{3}$

   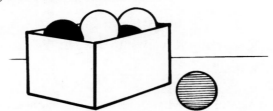

3. A magician puts two rabbits in a hat. One rabbit is black. One rabbit is brown. What is the probability of drawing the black rabbit out of the hat?

   a. $\frac{1}{2}$

   b. $\frac{1}{3}$

   c. $\frac{1}{4}$

4. Cade has four pairs of socks left in his drawer. One pair is white, one is black, one is tan, and one is green. If Cade reaches in his hand and without looking pulls out a pair of socks to wear, what is the probability that he will pull out the white pair?

   a. $\frac{1}{2}$

   b. $\frac{2}{4}$

   c. $\frac{1}{4}$

Money! Money! Money!

Most people use money every day, so it's important to know how to count, add, and subtract money. Different countries have different systems of money. In the United States we use coins that represent many different amounts.

1 cent	5 cents	10 cents	25 cents	50 cents
penny	nickel	dime	quarter	half dollar

Directions: Count to find each value. Write the answer on the line.

1. = _____

2. = _____

3. = _____

4. = _____

5. = _____

6. = _____

7. = _____

8. = _____

9. = _____

Spending Your Money

Directions: Look at the items in the pet store window, then read and answer each question. Be sure to show your work.

1. Macey has $5.00. She wants to buy a new puppy for her birthday. She also needs to buy a dish and a bag of dog food. How much money will she need? Does she have enough money to buy everything she wants? _____

2. Mrs. Kramer wants to buy a pet bird. She is going to buy a parrot and a bag of birdseed. How much money will Mrs. Kramer need?_____

3. Olivia is going to buy a frog for her English teacher and a gerbil for her science teacher. She has $1.20. How much more money does Olivia need to buy both gifts?_____

4. Calvin has been saving all of his change in his piggy bank. So far, he has saved $2.68. He wants to buy his dog Roscoe a new doghouse. How much more will he need to save before he can buy the doghouse? _____

Writing the Value

When you count money it is easiest if you start with the bill or coin that has the largest value. Of course, you should end with the bill or coin that has the smallest value.

To count this amount you should start with the 5 dollar bill, then add the 1 dollar bill, and finally add the 5 dimes. The total amount is $6.50.

Directions: Write each total amount.

1. _____

2. _____

3. _____

4. _____

5. _____

6. _____

7. _____

8. _____

9. _____

10. _____

Finding the Way

Directions: Complete each pattern.

1. 2, 4, 6, 8, _____, _____, _____

2. Z, Y, Z, Y, _____, _____, _____

3. ☐, ◯, △, ☐, _____, _____, _____

4. 20, 18, 16, 14, _____, _____, _____

5. 200, 300, 400, 500, _____, _____, _____

6. ◯◯, ☐☐, △△, ◯◯, _____, _____, _____

7. ☆☆, ☆☆☆☆, ☆☆, ☆☆☆☆, _____, _____, _____

8. 30, 31, 32, 33, _____, _____, _____

9. 987, 977, 967, 957, _____, _____, _____

10. , _____, _____, _____

11. X, Y, Z, X, _____, _____, _____

12. 2, 4, 8, 16, _____, _____, _____

13. A, AA, B, BB, C, _____, _____, _____

Can You Find the Pattern?

Part I

Directions: Finding patterns is like solving puzzles. See if you can match the patterns below. Draw a line from each pattern on the left to its partner on the right.

1. up, down, up   a. 40, 50, 60

2. 10, 20, 30,   b. W, V, U

3. blue, red, red   c. April, May, June

4. 9, 18, 27,   d. ?, !, ?

5. 20, 19, 18,   e. girl, boy, girl

6. Z, Y, X,   f. 500, 400, 300

7. January, February, March,   g. 17, 16, 15

8. boy, girl, boy,   h. blue, red, red

9. 800, 700, 600   i. 36, 45, 54

10. !, ?, !,   j. down, up, down

Part II

Directions: Complete each pattern.

1. 10 x 10, 11 x 11, 12 x 12, _____, _____, _____

2. ABC, DEF, GHI, _____, _____, _____

3. 1, 22, 333, _____, _____, _____

4. 25, 40, 55, _____, _____, _____

5. 1/4, 1/5, 1/6, _____, _____, _____

Inching Along

An *inch* is about the length of the tip of your finger. A ruler is 12 inches long. Inches are used to measure small items.

- 12 inches make one foot.
- A ruler is 12 inches, or one foot.
- Three feet make one yard.
- A yard stick is three feet or one yard.

Directions: Estimate the measurement of each item. Circle the correct answer.

1. an ant
   a. 1 inch
   b. 1 foot
   c. 1 yard

2. a picnic table
   a. 5 inches
   b. 5 feet
   c. 5 yards

3. a baseball glove
   a. 9 inches
   b. 9 feet
   c. 9 yards

4. a football field
   a. 100 inches
   b. 100 feet
   c. 100 yards

5. a donut
   a. 3 inches
   b. 3 feet
   c. 3 yards

6. a man
   a. 6 inches
   b. 6 feet
   c. 6 yards

How Long?

Directions: Use the measurement line to help find each length.

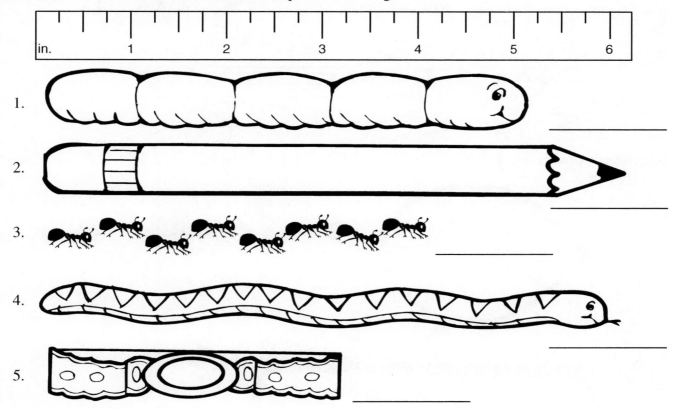

1. _____

2. _____

3. _____

4. _____

5. _____

Now it's your turn to draw.

6. Draw a piece of rope that is 4 inches long.

7. Draw a lizard that is 6 inches long.

8. Draw a bug that is 2 inches long.

9. Draw a piece of candy that is 1 inch long.

10. Draw a rectangle that is 5 inches long.

Metric Measuring

Centimeters and *decimeters* are used for measuring in the metric system. A centimeter is one of the smallest units of measurement in the metric system. A decimeter is equal to 10 centimeters.

1 centimeter = 10 decimeters

Part I

Directions: Draw a line to match each item to the closest measurement.

1.   5 cm

2.   7 cm

3.   1 dm

Part II

Directions: Draw a picture of your own that matches each measurement. Use the back of your paper, if needed.

4. 4 centimeters   7. 2 decimeters

5. 1 decimeter   8. 6 centimeters

6. 1 centimeter

Milliliters and Liters

Milliliters and *liters* are metric measurements. Milliliters are used to measure small amounts of liquid, and liters are used to measure larger amounts.

- mL = milliliter

- L = liter

- 1 liter = 1,000 milliliters

Directions: Choose the form you would use to measure each object. Circle the correct choice.

1. a bucket of water

   a. mL

   b. L

2. a glass of juice

   a. mL

   b. L

3. a pot of coffee

   a. mL

   b. L

4. a teaspoon of milk

   a. mL

   b. L

5. a pitcher of tea

   a. mL

   b. L

6. a laboratory beaker

   a. mL

   b. L

7. a child's swimming pool

   a. mL

   b. L

8. a mug of cider

   a. mL

   b. L

9. a dog's dish of water

   a. mL

   b. L

10. a baby's bottle

    a. mL

    b. L

More Ways to Measure

Cups, pints, quarts, and *gallons* are ways to measure liquids. When you want something warm and sweet to drink, you might have a cup of delicious, hot cocoa. When your parents put gas in their vehicles, they are putting gallons of gas in the tank. These units of measurement are important in your every day life.

Directions: Circle the correct measurement to show how you would measure each item.

1. Water in a pool
   a. cup
   b. gallon

2. Coffee in a mug
   a. cup
   b. quart

3. Lemonade in a pitcher
   a. pint
   b. gallon

4. Gasoline in a tank
   a. quart
   b. gallon

5. Tea in a glass
   a. cup
   b. quart

6. Water in a bathtub
   a. pint
   b. gallon

7. Sour cream in a container
   a. pint
   b. gallon

8. Oil in an engine
   a. cup
   b. quart

Weighing In

Ounces and *pounds* are units for measuring weight. When you go to the grocery you may notice the weight of the items listed on the packages. Sugar usually comes in 4 or 5 pound bags. Containers of yogurt are usually measured in ounces. Pay attention the weight of items you buy the next time you go on a shopping trip.

- oz. is the abbreviation for ounce
- lb. is the abbreviation for pound
- 16 oz. = 1 lb.

Part I

Directions: Decide which is larger, then write a greater than or less than sign (> or <).

1. 32 oz. _____ 1 lb.

2. 8 oz. _____ 8 lb.

3. 1 oz. _____ 1 lb.

4. 16 oz. _____ 1/2 lb.

5. 20 oz. _____ 3 lb.

6. 18 oz. _____ 2 lb.

Part II

Directions: Decide which measurement you would use to weigh each item, then circle your answer.

7. a feather
   a. ounce
   b. pound

8. a guitar
   a. ounce
   b. pound

9. a T-shirt
   a. ounce
   b. pound

10. a tire
    a. ounce
    b. pound

11. a yo yo
    a. ounce
    b. L

12. a couch
    a. ounce
    b. pound

13. an ink pen
    a. ounce
    b. pound

14. a snail
    a. ounce
    b. pound

15. a movie ticket
    a. ounce
    b. pound

16. a leaf
    a. ounce
    b. pound

Cold Enough for Snow?

Part I

Directions: Look at each thermometer. Write the temperature shown.

1. _____

2. _____

3. _____

4. _____

5. _____

6. _____

7. _____

8. _____

9. _____

Part II

Water freezes at 32 degrees, so when the temperature outside is 32 degrees or below, you might see snow. When the temperature outside is around 85 degrees or above, most people feel warm, so you might want to go swimming.

Directions Match each temperature to the correct event.

10. A heavy snow   98°F

11. A melting ice cream cone   40°F

12. A day when you might need a coat   70°F

13. The temperature in your home or school   30°F

Perfect Perimeter

The *perimeter* of an object is the distance around the object. To find the perimeter of an object, measure around the sides of the object and add the lengths together. The total measurement is the perimeter.

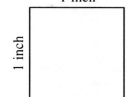

1 inch + 1 inch + 1 inch + 1 inch

Total perimeter: 4 inches

Directions: Use the sample ruler to help your draw each shape, then find the total perimeter. Use your own piece of paper or the back of this page if your need more room for each drawing.

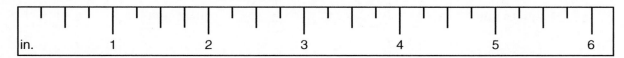

1. Draw a square with two-inch sides.

   Total perimeter:

2. Draw a triangle with three-inch sides.

   Total perimeter:

3. Draw a rectangle with two sides that are four inches long and two sides that are two inches long.

   Total perimeter:

4. Draw a square with one-inch sides.

   Total perimeter:

5. Draw a rectangle with two sides that are six inches long and two sides are three inches long.

   Total perimeter:

Something Extra: Draw a geometric figure of your own and find the perimeter.

Everywhere Area

Area is the number of square units in a particular space. To find the area of a shape, count the number of squares. The area for this figure is 11 square units.

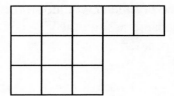

Part I

Directions: Find the area of each figure.

1. _____ square units

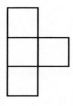

4. _____ square units

2. _____ square units

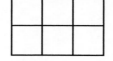

5. _____ square units

3. _____ square units

6. _____ square units

Part II

Directions: Draw a figure that has the number of square units given.

7. 8 square units

10. 9 square units

8. 12 square units

11. 14 square units

9. 2 square units

12. 15 square units

Ship Shape

Directions: Look at the picture of the ship. Find and color each shape listed below.

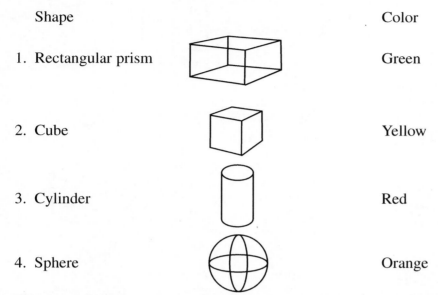

Shape	Color
1. Rectangular prism	Green
2. Cube	Yellow
3. Cylinder	Red
4. Sphere	Orange

Something Extra: Draw two cone shapes somewhere on your ship. Color the cones blue.

Name the Shape

Directions: Name the shape of each figure. Choose from the list below.

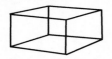

rectangular prism   cube   cylinder   sphere   cone

1. a witch's hat

6. an ice cream cone

2. dice

7. a hat box

3. a shoe box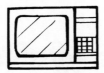

8. children's wooden blocks

4. a microwave oven

9. a can of soup

5. a baseball

10. a soccer ball

Now it's your turn. In the space below, draw an example of each shape.

sphere	cube	rectangular prism

Plane Figures

The outline of a shape forms a *plane figure*.

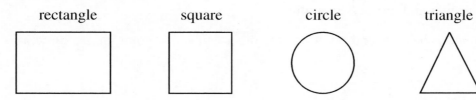

| rectangle | square | circle | triangle |

Directions: In the space below, draw a picture using only plane figures. Your shapes can be all different sizes. Be sure to color your picture when you are finished.

Getting On Line

A *line* is straight with no end point. It goes on forever in both directions.

A *line segment* is straight and has two end points.

A *ray* is part of a line. It has one end point and the other end keeps going in one direction.

Part I

Directions: Circle the name of each figure.

1.   ●━━━━●

   a. line segment

   b. line

   c. ray

2.   ●━━━━▶

   a. line segment

   b. line

   c. ray

3.   ◀━━━━●

   a. line segment

   b. line

   c. ray

4.   ◀━━━━▶

   a. line segment

   b. line

   c. ray

Part II

Directions: Draw each picture.

5. Draw a sun with 10 rays.

6. Draw a house, using 6 to 8 line segments.

7. Draw a spider with 8 rays for legs.

It's All in the Angle

Two rays with a common end point form an *angle*. The common end point is called a *vertex*. An angle that forms the shape of an L or a square corner is called a *right angle*.

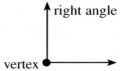

Part I

Directions: Look around the room. List at least 6 examples of right angles that you see.

    For example: The corner of a fish tank

1.

2.

3.

4.

5.

6.

Part II

Directions: Look at each figure. Write *yes* if the figure is an angle. Write *no* if the figure is not an angle.

7. _____

10. _____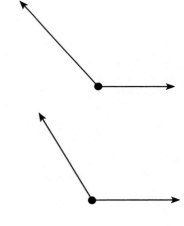

8. _____

11. _____

9. _____

2. _____

It's All the Same

Figures that are *congruent* are the same size and shape. Congruent figures can be turned in any direction and still be congruent.

Examples: Congruent   Not Congruent

Directions: Use the graph below to draw eight sets of figures that are congruent.

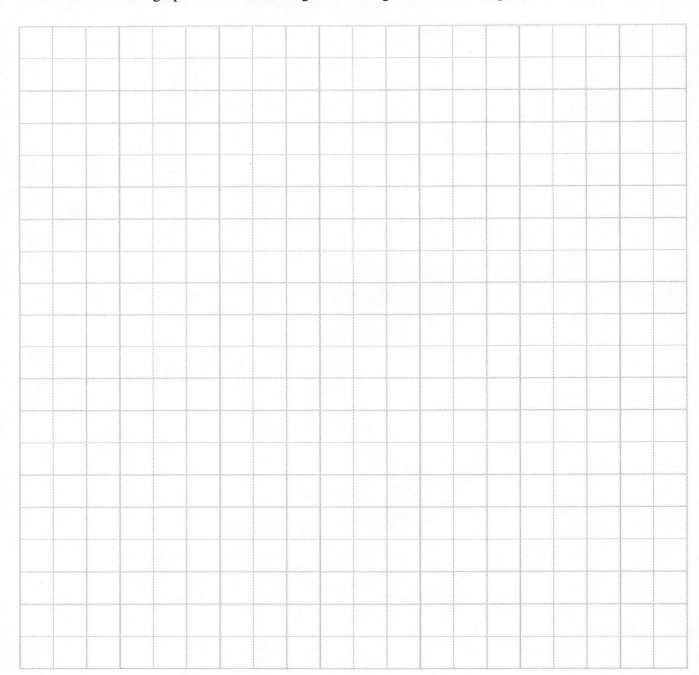

Congruent: Big Word, Easy Idea

When objects are *congruent* they are the same size and the same shape, no matter which way they are turned.

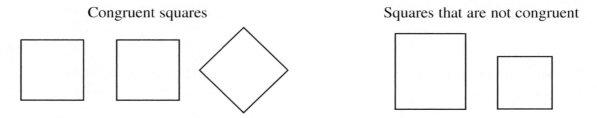

Congruent squares   Squares that are not congruent

Directions: Look at the picture below. Find the 20 congruent shapes and color each of the 10 pairs the same color. Remember to change colors for each new pair.

Perfect Symmetry

A *line of symmetry* divides a shape so that the two halves of the figure mirror each other across the line, like this.

If you folded a shape along a line of symmetry, both sides would fit exactly together. Here are some symmetrical objects:

These objects are not symmetrical:

Part I

Directions: Draw the line or lines of symmetry for each shape.

1.

2.

3.

4.

5.

Part II

Directions: Draw six shapes of your own. Decide if each shape is symmetrical. If it is, draw the line or lines of symmetry and write the word *symmetrical*. If it is not, write the words *no symmetry*.

Art and Symmetry

A figure that has *symmetry* can be folded in two so that the two parts match exactly.

Directions: Many artists use symmetry in their drawings and paintings. Now it's your turn to try. Look at each picture half. Draw the other half of the picture so that it is perfectly symmetrical.

When you are finished color each of your pictures, as any good artist would. Then, cut out each picture and try folding it on its line of symmetry.

1.

2.

3.

4.

Tick Tock

Time is important to everyone. See how good you are at telling time by completing the exercise below.

Directions: Look at each clock and write the time.

Time to Tell Time

Part I

Directions: Match each time below.

1. seven thirty	a. 9:00
2. eight fifteen	b. 7:30
3. nine o'clock	c. 12:00
4. five fifteen	d. 8:15
5. twelve noon	e. 5:15

Part II

Directions: Draw the time given on the empty clock face.

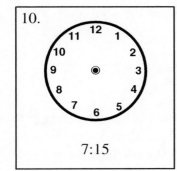

6.

3:15

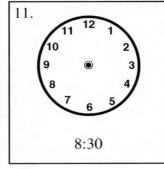

7.

8:00

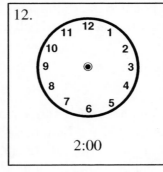

8.

9:30

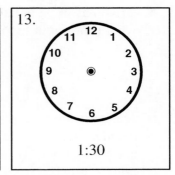

9.

12:00

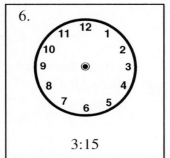

10.

7:15

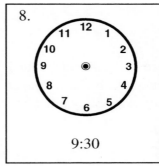

11.

8:30

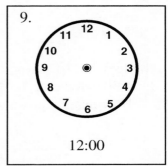

12.

2:00

13.

1:30

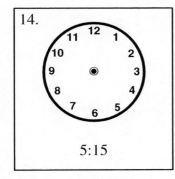

14.

5:15

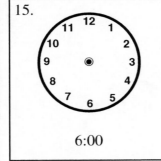

15.

6:00

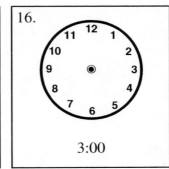

16.

3:00

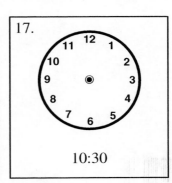

17.

10:30

Working with Time

Directions: Read and solve each word problem.

1. Margie has to be at the dentist at 6:00 o'clock. She gets off work at 4:00 o'clock. When Margie is finished with work, how much time does she have before she has to be at the dentist?

2. School starts at 7:15 in the morning. Heath's alarm goes off at 6:15 in the morning. How much time does Heath have each morning before he has to be at school?

3. Mary put her brownies in the oven at 3:00. The directions on the box said to bake the brownies for 45 minutes. At what time should Mary take the brownies out of the oven?

4. Suzy has soccer practice every Tuesday and Thursday. On Tuesday she practices from 3:00 until 4:00. However, on Thursday she has a longer practice, and she practices from 3:00 until 5:00. How many hours a week does Suzy practice soccer?

5. Brian has to be at ball practice in 30 minutes. The clock says that it is 2:15 in the afternoon. At what time should Brian arrive at the baseball park?

6. Jeanne is hungry. She and her friend Tara usually eat lunch at 11:00, but Tara is late. Jeanne decides she will wait until 1:00 for Tara, but if Tara is not ready to eat by 1:00, then Jeanne will eat without her. If Jeanne waits till 1:00 to eat, and she usually eats at 11:00, how far past her regular lunchtime will she be eating her lunch?

Not All Time Looks the Same

Not all clocks look the same. Some clocks have an hour and a minute hand. Some clocks, or watches, are smaller and made to wear on your arm. Some clocks are digital — this means there is no hour or minute hand. Instead, the time is shown with numerals, with the hour showing first and then the minute, separated by a colon.

Directions: Look at each time piece and write or draw the hour and minute to show what time you do each activity.

1. This is the time I wake-up for school.

2. This is the time I eat my breakfast.

3. This is the time I get to school.

4. This is the time I eat lunch.

5. This is the time I have math class.

6. This is the time I get home from school.

7. This is the time I play outside or watch some television.

8. This is the time I eat supper.

9. This is the time I start getting ready for bed.

10. This is the time on a school night that I go to bed.

Learning About Graphs

A *graph* is a way to organize information. A *bar graph* is a graph that uses bar shapes to give information about a topic.

Look at the following graph. This graph shows how much television Michael, Jana, Kevin, and Alicia watch each day.

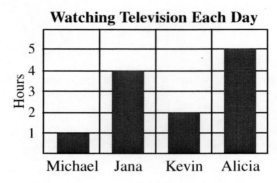

Michael watches the least television. He watches 1 hour each day.

Alicia watches the most television. She watches 5 hours each day.

What are some other things you know from looking at this graph?

Part I

Directions: Look at the bar graph and answer the questions below.

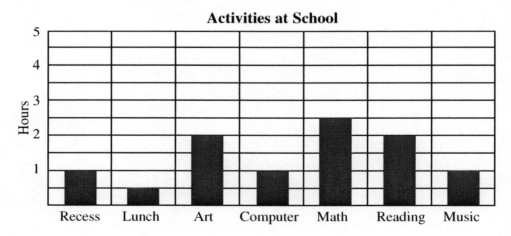

1. How many hours is math class? _____

2. How long is recess? _____

3. Which is longer, music class or reading class? How do you know? _____

4. Which class is as long as reading class? _____

5. Which class or activity is the longest? _____

6. What activity or class is the shortest? _____

Graphing Your Own Day

A *bar graph* is a visual way to give information. Look at the example below.

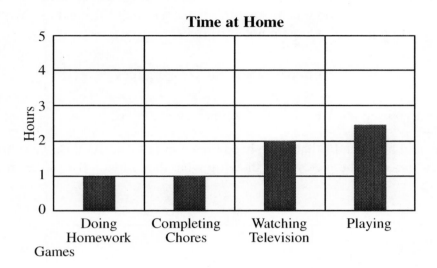

Directions: Make a bar graph of your own to show the information below. The outline of the graph is already drawn for you.

- Be sure to give your graph a title.

- Label the times on the left side of your graph.

- Label each activity across the bottom of your graph.

- You must list at least five activities that you do during the day.

Picture This

A *pictograph* uses pictures to represent numbers of objects. A pictograph has a *key* to show what each symbol represents. For example, if someone tried to draw a pictograph showing the number of trees in a large forest, it would take up too much paper to draw every tree. Instead, the writer would use a symbol, such as a tree, to represent a large number of trees.

1 tree symbol = 20 trees

This shows that when you see one tree, it actually represents 20 trees.

Directions: Tristan and his friend Ethan have been on a nature hike. As they were hiking they saw many different birds. Look at the pictograph showing what they saw on their hike and answer the questions below.

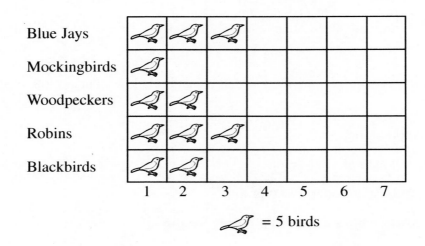

= 5 birds

1. Which bird did they see the most? _____

2. Which bird did they see the least?_____

3. How many blue jays did they see? _____

4. How many total woodpeckers and blackbirds did they see?_____

5. How many birds did they see in all? _____

6. Pretend they saw 20 blackbirds on their trip. Draw the symbol or symbols needed on the graph to show this many blackbirds.

Fun in the Sun

Directions: A survey was taken at Cheatham Middle School to see where the students liked to take their vacations. The pictograph below shows how many students voted for each place. One sun represents three votes. Use the pictograph to answer the questions.

Sunny Vacation Spots	
Panama City	☀ ☀ ☀ ☀ ☀
Myrtle Beach	☀ ☀ ☀
Gulf Shores	☀ ☀ ☀ ☀
Virginia Beach	☀ ☀ ☀
Cancun	☀ ☀

☀ = 3 votes

1. Which vacation spot received the most votes? _____

2. How many students voted for it? _____

3. Which two vacation spots tied? _____

4. How many votes did these two receive? _____

5. Which vacation spot received the least number of votes? _____

6. How many votes did it receive? _____

7. How many more votes did Panama City receive than Cancun? _____

8. According to the pictograph, how many total votes were represented? _____

Tally Ho!

One way to collect numerical information is to use *tally marks*. Each slash or tally mark represents a number. If you want to show the number 3 using tally marks, then you make three slashes: / / /.

If two teams are playing a game, you can keep score using tally marks.

The Reds   The Whites

| | | ʮʮʮ | |

Look at the score for the second team. They have a score of 7. When you are tallying and you get to the number 5, always make a slash or tally mark that goes across the previous 4 marks, creating a group of five. Then, you start a new group of tally marks. Why? This makes your marks easier to count because you can count by fives.

Directions: Use tally marks to show each amount. Remember to group by 5's whenever you can.

1. The number of letters in the name of the city where you live.

2. The number of letters in your last name.

3. The number of people in your classroom. (And yes, the teacher counts as a person.)

4. The number of times you usually eat during the day.

5. The number of days in the month of December.

6. The number of people in your family.

7. The number of days in a week.

8. The number of boys in your class.

Measuring Time in the Past

Directions: When you study history, you measure time in different ways depending on how long ago an event happened. Look at each event and circle which time measurement you would use to tell how long ago each event happened.

one year = 365 days

one decade = ten years

one century = 100 years or ten decades

1. Your birth	years	decades	centuries
2. When dinosaurs lived	years	decades	centuries
3. Your grandparents' births	years	decades	centuries
4. The Ice Age	years	decades	centuries
5. The 1950's	years	decades	centuries
6. The Pilgrims' landing at Plymouth	years	decades	centuries
7. Your second birthday	years	decades	centuries
8. Your first doctor's appointment	years	decades	centuries
9. Your parents' first day at school	years	decades	centuries
10. Your first day at school	years	decades	centuries
11. When public school first began	years	decades	centuries
12. When there were wooly mammoths	years	decades	centuries
13. When there was no electricity	years	decades	centuries
14. When video games were first invented	years	decades	centuries
15. Your earliest, happy memory	years	decades	centuries

Time Lines

Directions: Look at the time line and answer the questions below.

Princess, a Dog's Life

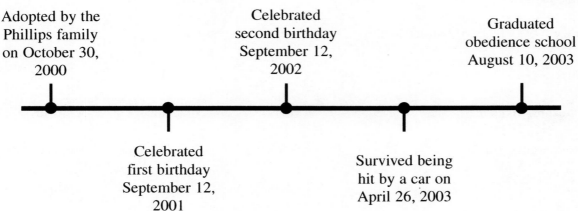

1. When did Princess celebrate her first birthday? _____

2. How old (in years and months) was Princess when she was hit by the car? _____

3. Between which two events do you think Princess entered obedience school?

   _____

4. When did Princess graduate from obedience school? _____

This is Your Life

Part I

Directions: List, in order of occurrence, some of the major events in your life. For example, when were you born? What's your earliest memory? When did you lose your fist tooth? Have you ever broken a bone? Have you received any major awards? If you need more space, use the back of this paper.

1. _____

2. _____

3. _____

4. _____

5. _____

6. _____

7. _____

8. _____

Part II

Directions: Look over your list of major events. Now choose at least six of these and write these events on the time line below.

_____'s Life

(Your name)

The First Colonies

Directions: Look at the time line and then answer the questions

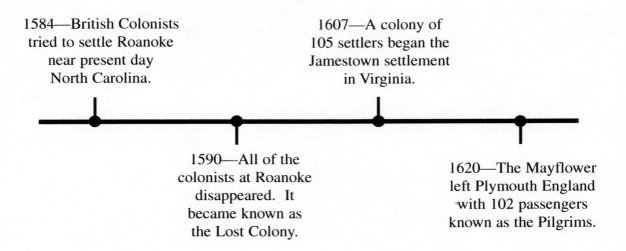

1584—British Colonists tried to settle Roanoke near present day North Carolina.

1607—A colony of 105 settlers began the Jamestown settlement in Virginia.

1590—All of the colonists at Roanoke disappeared. It became known as the Lost Colony.

1620—The Mayflower left Plymouth England with 102 passengers known as the Pilgrims.

1. When was the first successful colony established in America? _____

2. What happened to the colonists at Roanoke? _____

3. What colony was founded in 1607? _____

4. Who arrived on the Mayflower in 1620? _____

Past, Present, and Future

Directions: Look at each invention or possible invention. Decide if it is an invention that was used in the past, an invention that is used in the present, or an invention that might be used in the future. Circle your answer.

1. a spinning wheel   past   present   future

2. satellite television   past   present   future

3. cars that fly in the air   past   present   future

4. telephones with caller identification   past   present   future

5. a butter churn   past   present   future

6. cellular phones   past   present   future

7. robots working as maids in every home   past   present   future

8. notebook computers   past   present   future

Something Extra: Think of an invention that you currently use and try to improve it for the future. How would you change it? How would you make it better? Why would you need to improve it? Draw a picture of your new invention.

My, How Things Change

Directions: Look at how people did things in the past or how they do them in the present, and then fill in the information that is missing in each column.

1. In the past people used the pony express to deliver their mail.	Now people use
2. In the past people used a telegraph to send information quickly.	Now people use
3. In the past people used _____ to travel.	Now people use cars for most of their daily travel.
4. In the past people used _____ to help them see when it was dark.	Now most people use electric lights.
5. In the past people used big cooking pots over open fires to cook their food.	Now people use
6. In the past people used passenger trains to travel across the country.	Now people use
7. In the past people used boats powered by the wind.	Now more people use
8. In the past people used _____ to record thoughts and ideas.	Now people write their thoughts more quickly using personal computers.

Tales through the Ages

Directions: Diaries and journals were often used to record important memories. Without the written memories of people of the past, there would be much we would not know about what their lives were like and how they lived.

Write a journal entry about your life to be read by people in the future. Describe the things you do each day and any electronic equipment that is important in your life. Write about school and your friends and what you do for entertainment. Remember, you are writing this entry for people in the future who may not be familiar with this time, so be sure to use plenty of detail and description.

_____

_____

_____

_____

_____

_____

_____

_____

_____

_____

_____

_____

The Brave Settlers

Directions: Many brave settlers of the past paved the way for today's communities, such as Nashville, Tennessee. Look at the events of the city's history and place them in order by writing the numbers 1–5 under each picture and its description.

1.
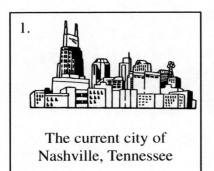
The current city of
Nashville, Tennessee

_____

2.
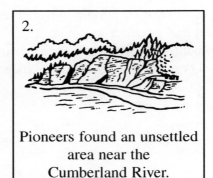
Pioneers found an unsettled
area near the
Cumberland River.

_____

3.

Early settlers built
Fort Nashboro.

_____

4.

Richard Henderson
purchased land from the
Cherokee in 1775

_____

5.

Despite early attacks, the
settlement managed
to thrive.

_____

Something extra: Many early communities or settlements were begun on the banks of rivers. List some reasons why you think early settlers would have chosen to build near a river.

_____

_____

_____

_____

_____

_____

_____

_____

How Communities Change

Directions: Over time communities change and grow. Look at the picture of this pioneer town and answer the questions below.

1. What are some things that are different about the school in the pioneer town and the school you attend? _____

   _____

2. How is today's transportation different from transportation in the past? _____

3. List three ways you think towns or cities of today are better than towns or cities of the past.

   _____

   _____

   _____

4. In the space below draw a picture of your own town. Be sure to color your picture.

The First Settlers

When Columbus found the Americas in 1492, there were settlers already present. These early settlers were called Indians because Columbus mistakenly thought he had landed in India, the land he was trying to reach. Actually, these Indians were made up of many different tribes with many different names, beliefs, and traditions. How these Indians lived was, in many ways, a result of where they lived. For example, the Plains lived in tepees so they could easily move while hunting buffalo. The Cherokee Indians adopted a more settled environment and tried to fit in with the white settlers.

Directions: Read each statement and write *true* if the answer is true and *false* if the answer is false.

1. _____ Columbus and his men were the first settlers in America.

2. _____ All Indians lived in similar communities.

3. _____ The Indians were really the first Americans.

4. _____ Columbus called the Indians "Indians" because he thought he'd landed in Australia.

5. _____ The Indian tribes arrived with Columbus.

6. _____ Plains Indians lived in tepees because they were easy to move.

7. _____ Columbus is given credit for discovering the Americas.

8. _____ Columbus was trying to find the Americas in 1492.

9. _____ The Cherokee Indians roamed all over the Americas.

10. _____ None of the Indian tribes tried to get along with the new settlers.

Planning Their Routes

Most early explorers decided their routes based on the land forms surrounding them. For example, rather than passing over a large mountain, the early explorers would try to find a gap or pass through the mountain.

Directions: Look at the landform map below. Use the map key to help you identify the various land forms. Color the land forms according to the key.

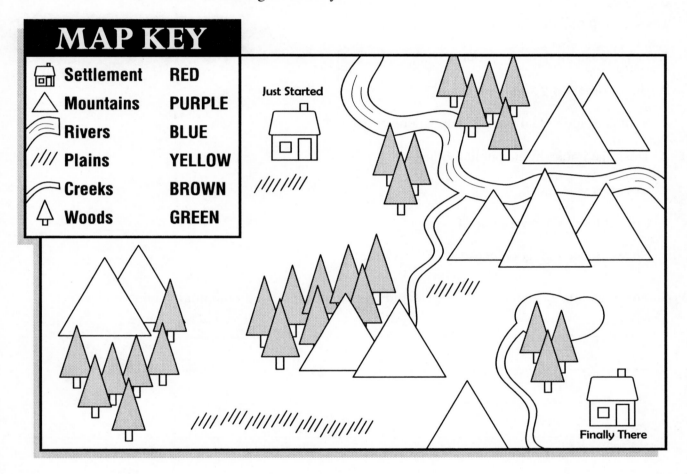

When you are finished coloring, draw a line on the map to show the easiest route from the settlement of Just Started to the settlement of Finally There. On the back of this sheet, explain why this is the easiest route.

Community Helpers

Directions: Today there are many ways people can help improve their own communities. Look at the list of activities below and circle the choices that would help a community.

1. Build homes for the poor.

2. Keep the environment clean.

3. Help stop pollution.

4. Leave trash all over the ground.

5. Have community volunteer days.

6. Volunteer individual time to help wherever needed.

7. Trash the books in the public library.

8. Never recycle.

9. Collect food for those in need.

10. Never donate to a good cause.

What are some things someone your age could do to help make your community a better place?

11. _____

_____

_____

12. _____

_____

_____

13. _____

_____

_____

14. _____

_____

_____

Celebrating the Past

Directions: Many communities have special days to celebrate events from the past. These festivals usually become yearly events where members of the community gather to remember what life was once like in their community and how things have changed.

Imagine you were asked to create a special day of celebration for your school community. What would you name the event? How would you celebrate? What date would you choose? What special people would you want to recognize? What special activities would take place at your event?

Use the above questions to help you plan a poster to advertise the special day.

Welcome to the 1st Annual _____ **Festival**

Life in an Indian Village

Directions: Read the story about life in an Indian village and then answer the questions below.

The Powhatan Indians were a group of Native Americans who lived near what became the early Jamestown Settlement in Virginia. The Powhatan were a settled community that lived in villages. Most had longhouses where their families lived. These houses had indoor fires for warmth during the cold, winter months. Their homes also had storage shelves to keep food and other items safely tucked away.

Everyone in the village had a job and most of their activities centered around daily survival. The women of the village helped take care of the crops. They harvested such foods as corn, beans, and squash. They also ate other foods such as roots, berries, and grains. Many of these foods would be dried and saved to eat during the long, winter months. The men used spears, traps, and nets to capture animals for food and clothing. They used their nets to capture animals from the nearby ocean.

Children were also an important part of the village. They helped their parents wherever needed. However, the Powhatan children were also allowed to play and have fun. One game they played, that children still play today, was dress up. They would dress in their parents' clothes and adorn themselves with paint and jewelry.

Life in the Powhatan village was a lot of work, but there was also much fun to be had in the Indian community.

1. Tell at least two ways that life in the Powhatan village is similar to life in a modern day community._____

   _____

   _____

2. What was the main job of the women in the village? _____

   _____

   _____

3. Were the Powhatan a settled tribe or a nomad (wandering) tribe? How do you know?

   _____

   _____

4. If you lived in the Powhatan village what do you think would be some of the jobs you would be expected to do? _____

   _____

5. What was the main job of the men in the Powhatan village?_____

   _____

Which Way Do We Go?

When the early settlers landed in the original 13 colonies, one problem that faced them was deciding which direction they would go. It is important to know the directions of North, South, West, and East when planning any journey.

Directions: Use the compass rose and the map below to help you answer the following questions. Circle your answer.

1. If an early settler landed in Virginia which direction would he or she need to go to reach Maryland?

   a. southeast

   b. east

   c. north

2. For a colonist living in Massachusetts, the Atlantic Ocean would be located to the

   a. south

   b. east

   c. west

3. How many colonies on the map are south of Maryland?

   a. two

   b. three

   c. one

4. How many colonies on the map are north of Virginia?

   a. eight

   b. six

   c. four

5. According to the map, Rhode Island is located _____ of New Jersey.

   a. southwest

   b. northeast

   c. northwest

What's Pretty to You?

Geography is the study of the different areas of the earth. When the first explorers came to America they encountered many different types of geography. They used the land types to help them decide where to settle. In some ways people still do this today, but people also like to live in geographic areas that appeal to them

Directions: Draw and color a picture of each geographic feature. Then, circle the picture where you would most like to live. In the space provided, explain why you would want to live in this area.

1. Desert	2. Forest
3. Mountains	4. Ocean

I would most like to live near _____ because _____

_____

_____

_____ .

13 Important Colonies

As America became filled with more and more people wanting to settle in the new world, towns began to grow. Eventually these areas were divided into 13 colonies.

Directions: Label each of the 13 colonies on the map below. Then color each colony a different color. Use the word bank to help you.

Word bank

Virginia	Massachusetts	New York	Maryland
Rhode Island	Connecticut	Delaware	Georgia
New Hampshire	North Carolina	South Carolina	New Jersey
Pennsylvania			

The Thirteen Colonies

Knowing a Legend

One of the first things early settlers needed to do was identify the area where they were. One way they did this was by drawing maps. Maps help show locations. Maps also use symbols to help identify certain features. The meanings of the symbols can be found inside the map's legend.

Directions: Look at the legend below. What do you think each symbol means? Write your answer beside each symbol.

1.
_____

2.
_____

3.
_____

4.
_____

5.
_____

6.
_____

7.
_____

8.
_____

Now it's your turn. Draw the missing symbols inside the legend

School

Hospital

Bridge

Oh, Pioneers!

As the United States grew and the eastern states became crowded, many people wanted to move out West. These brave explorers became known as *pioneers*.

Directions: Look at each item below. Circle and color only the items that might have belonged to pioneers.

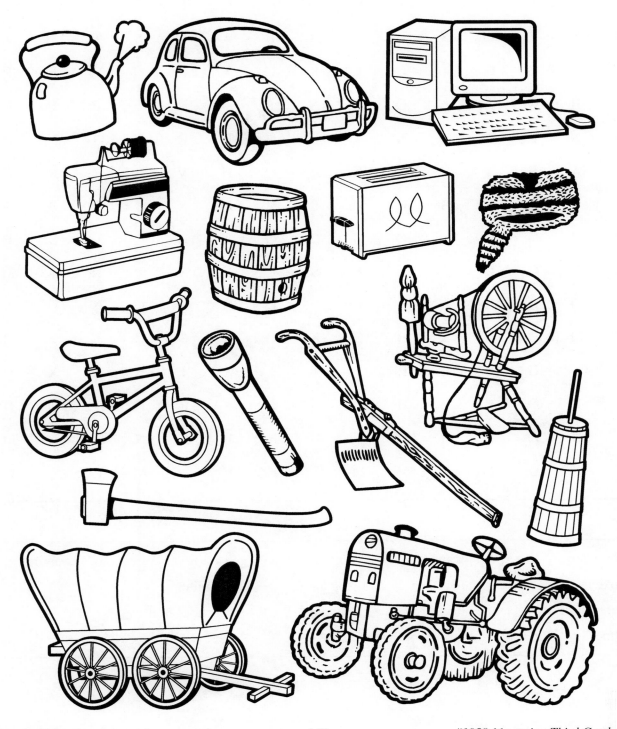

Pioneer Word Search

Directions: Search for words connected to the early pioneers. Words may be hidden vertically, horizontal, or diagonally. Use the word bank to help you in your search.

H	Q	P	N	D	R	W	D	C	O	P	C	X	V	U
Q	Y	I	O	X	B	P	A	B	A	C	S	F	M	Z
N	S	O	G	T	C	K	K	C	X	E	O	W	E	P
I	B	N	A	E	O	H	N	F	D	X	B	R	F	C
F	N	E	W	R	N	I	V	H	B	R	L	J	N	H
L	W	E	T	U	K	K	L	Q	H	V	E	I	R	Q
I	O	R	M	S	U	U	L	P	D	X	J	P	B	I
H	H	G	N	S	C	H	O	O	L	H	O	U	S	E
B	T	O	C	Z	L	E	S	L	F	S	P	R	I	M
L	O	R	X	A	S	E	L	D	N	A	C	N	D	N
C	M	D	A	K	B	O	K	O	C	S	D	E	R	P
M	G	G	B	E	E	I	I	X	W	I	E	U	X	U
C	R	O	P	S	H	L	N	E	A	R	H	Y	Q	B
J	B	Z	F	S	C	V	U	N	P	C	N	L	L	M
V	X	D	E	I	V	M	S	H	E	H	M	O	Q	A

pioneer	wagon	ax	corn	churn
oxen	hearth	log cabin	Indians	
coonskin cap	deer	candles	school house	
hoe	crops			

The Trail of Tears

Directions: Read the story below and answer the questions.

The Cherokee Indians had adapted a way of life much like the European settlers who had become their neighbors. They lived in settled villages, had an organized system of government, and even had a written alphabet that had been developed by a Cherokee Indian known by the name of Sequoyah. However, when gold was found in Georgia, the settlers became greedy and wanted more land, including the land held by the Cherokees.

In 1830, under President Andrew Jackson, Congress passed the Indian Removal Act. The Cherokee were forced to leave their homes and were made to march across the country to Oklahoma. Thousands of Cherokees died during this march that has since become known as the Trail of Tears.

1. Describe how the Cherokee Indians lived. _____

   _____

   _____

2. Who created the Cherokee alphabet? _____

   _____

3. Why did settlers suddenly want the Cherokee's land? _____

   _____

4. Who was president during this time? _____

5. What act did Congress pass to remove the Cherokees? _____

6. Where were the Cherokee Indians being forced to go? _____

7. What happened to many of the Cherokee during the journey? _____

   _____

8. What is this journey known as today? _____

9. Why do you think it is called this? _____

   _____

10. Do you think it was right for the government to remove the Cherokee from their land? Why or why not? _____

   _____

   _____

Folk Heroes and Legends

As pioneers spread into the colonies and then west into other areas of what are now the United States, many folk heroes became known for their daring deeds and bravery. Some of the best known folk heroes and legends were real people such as Sacajawea, Pocahontas, Daniel Boone, and Davy Crockett. Sacajawea was known for helping Lewis and Clark lead their expedition. Pocahontas helped the colonists at Jamestown when she formed a friendship with Captain John Smith. Daniel Boone and Davy Crockett were both known for their bravery as they headed into unknown territories.

Directions: Imagine you are an early pioneer headed out west. What brave deeds might you do to become a legend? Where would you go? Why would you go there? What famous people would you hope to meet on your journey?

In the space below write a short paragraph about your adventures, and on the back of this page, draw a picture of yourself as an early pioneer.

_____

_____

_____

_____

_____

_____

_____

_____

_____

_____

_____

The Importance of Geography

If you looked at a map of the original 13 colonies, you would see they were located near the Atlantic Ocean. This allowed the settlers easy access to waterways for shipping, transportation, and food. Most settlements were located in certain geographical regions for specific reasons.

Directions: Think about each type of geographical location and give reasons why settlers might have located there.

1. On an island _____

_____

_____

_____

2. In the mountains _____

_____

_____

_____

3. Near a lake _____

_____

_____

_____

4. In the grassy plains _____

_____

_____

_____

5. Near a river _____

_____

_____

_____

The Declaration of Independence

Directions: Read the story below and answer each question.

The original 13 colonies were tired of being ruled by England. They wanted to make their own laws, but the King of England would not listen to them. Because of their unending disagreements, the colonists decided to go to war against England. This war became known as the Revolutionary War.

As the colonists organized themselves for war, many great men emerged as leaders. Men like Ben Franklin, Thomas Jefferson, and Paul Revere would all help to fight the British. Thomas Jefferson is also known for writing the Declaration of Independence. This document declared to the world that the colonies wanted to be free from England. It listed all the reasons they believed England was hurting the colonies and why the colonies should be free. The Declaration of Independence was adopted on July 4, 1776. This date would later be known as America's birthday.

1. How many original colonies were there? _____

2. Who ruled the original 13 colonies? _____

3. Why did the colonies want to be free from England? _____

   _____

   _____

4. What war was fought between the colonies and England? _____

5. Name two famous leaders for the colonists. _____

6. Who wrote the Declaration of Independence? _____

7. What was the Declaration of Independence? _____

8. On what date was the Declaration of Independence adopted? _____

9. What would this date later be known as? _____

10. Do you think the men who wrote and signed the Declaration of Independence were brave? Why or why not? _____

   _____

   _____

   _____

Know Your Stuff

Directions: Read each statement. Decide if the statement is true or false. Then write your answer on the line provided.

_____ 1. A tax is money that is owed to a government.

_____ 2. The Civil War was the name of the war fought between the 13 colonies and England.

_____ 3. George Washington was the first President of the United States.

_____ 4. The early colonists wrote the Declaration of Independence to state the reasons why they wanted longer vacation breaks.

_____ 5. A constitution is a document that lists a government's powers and its citizen's rights.

_____ 6. There were 15 original colonies.

_____ 7. Those who first came to settle in America were known as colonists.

_____ 8. The original 13 colonies were governed by England until after the Revolutionary War.

_____ 9. Many people came to the colonies because they wanted freedom of religion.

_____ 10. Those colonists who fought for freedom in the Revolutionary War were called Indians.

The Original Stars and Stripes

When the Revolutionary War was fought, the colonies needed a flag they could use to represent them as one unit. Up until this time each colony had its own flag, but this would no longer do since they were all fighting for freedom against England. Betsy Ross made the first flag using the suggestions given to her by George Washington.

Directions: Below is a picture of the original flag. Color the flag according to the directions and then answer the questions.

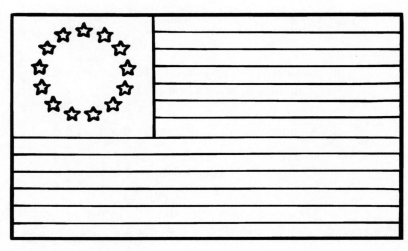

- Color the 13 stripes red and white. The top and bottom stripes should be red.

- Color the square blue.

- Color the stars white.

1. Who was Betsy Ross? _____

_____

_____

2. Why does the flag have 13 stripes? _____

_____

_____

3. Who helped design the flag? _____

_____

_____

4. Why does the country's flag look different now? _____

_____

_____

The American Flag

Directions: Color the American flag according to the directions and then answer the questions below.

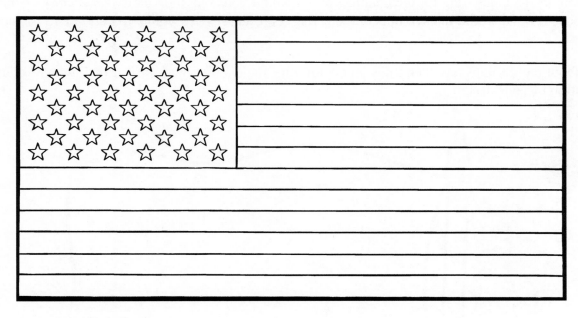

- Color the stripes red and white. The top and bottom stripes should be red.
- Color the square blue.
- Color the stars white.

1. Why are there 50 stars on the flag? _____

_____

_____

2. Why are there 13 stripes? _____

_____

_____

3. What 3 colors are used for the flag? _____

_____

_____

4. What do you think the flag is a symbol of? _____

_____

_____

Design Your Own Flag

Directions: Using what you know about the United States of America, its past and its present, see if you can design a new flag for the country. What would your flag look like? What colors would you choose? What would the symbols on your flag represent? Why would you choose to use certain symbols?

Think about these things and then draw and color your flag. When you are finished, write a brief explanation of your design.

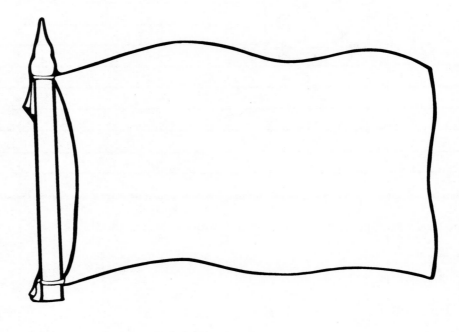

_____

_____

_____

_____

_____

_____

_____

_____

_____

_____

Knowing the Pledge

Directions: The Pledge to the Flag was written by Francis Bellamy. Look at the pledge below and see if you can explain the lines that are so often recited.

1. **I pledge allegiance to the Flag**

   What this means to you: _____

   _____

   _____

   _____

2. **of the United States of America,**

   What this means to you: _____

   _____

   _____

   _____

3. **and to the Republic for which it stands,**

   What this means to you: _____

   _____

   _____

   _____

4. **one Nation under God, indivisible,**

   What this means to you: _____

   _____

   _____

5. **with liberty and justice for all.**

   What this means to you: _____

   _____

   _____

Who or What is That?

Directions: Write the letter of each well-known picture on the line next to its name.

1. the Statue of Liberty _____

a.

2. Betsy Ross _____

b.

3. an eagle _____

c.

4. Ben Franklin _____

d.

5. George Washington _____

e.

6. the Capitol building _____

f.

7. the White House _____

g.

8. the Liberty Bell _____

h.

9. the Lincoln Memorial _____

i.

10. Abraham Lincoln _____

j.

The Right to Protest

The early colonists did not like England putting a tax on goods when the colonists did not vote for the tax. To fight "taxation without representation" the colonists decided to protest. Dressed as Indians, colonists snuck onto English ships and threw boxes of taxed tea into the waters of Boston Harbor. This protest later became known as the Boston Tea Party.

Directions: Imagine your principal has just decided that all the students at your school must bring only peanut butter and jelly sandwiches every day for lunch. You may have no chips or hot meals, and for your drink you must bring water every day. And he or she has forbidden all desserts!

Imagine you are going to organize a protest of the students in your classroom. Why are you protesting? Why do you believe the situation is unfair? What can you do to get your point across to the principal? What do you think will happen if you protest? Would you need to disguise yourself as the colonists did? How will you get your classmates to agree to protest? Use these questions to help you write about the day you organized a protest about the new school lunches.

_____

_____

_____

_____

_____

_____

_____

_____

_____

_____

_____

_____

American Democracy

Directions: Read each statement below. Circle each statement that shows a basic principle of American democracy.

1. All people are created equal.

2. The United States of America should have a king or a queen.

3. Everyone is innocent until proven guilty.

4. Everyone has the right to pursue happiness.

5. Only the rich have the right to pursue happiness.

6. All people should have freedom of religion.

7. The citizens should not have freedom of speech.

8. The government should have no limits with its power.

9. All people should have equal opportunities.

10. No one can speak out against the government

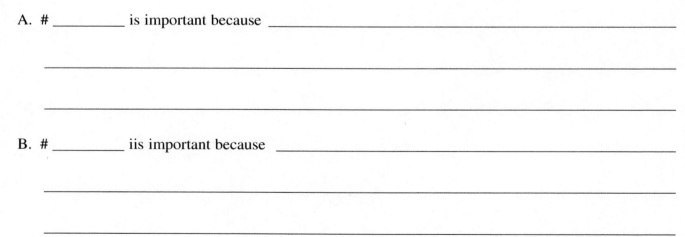

Choose any two of the statements you circled and explain why these are important principles of democracy.

A. # _____ is important because _____

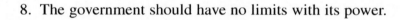

_____

B. # _____ iis important because _____

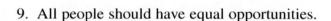

_____

Women's Right to Vote

In America, every citizen aged 18 or older has the right to vote, but everyone did not always have that right. Susan B. Anthony worked for years to give women the right to vote. Finally after many years, she helped win that right when the 19th amendment was added to the Constitution.

Directions: Imagine you are trying to get all people the right to vote. Create a campaign poster that tells why everyone should be able to vote—including people your own age.

1. Why do you think people your age are not included in the right to vote? _____

    _____

    _____

2. Do you think the reasons are fair? _____

    _____

    _____

3. Why do you think women were not originally given the right to vote? _____

    _____

4. Do you know of any other people who were denied the right to vote in America's past?

    _____

    _____

Promised Equality

Sojourner Truth was born a slave. She ran away just before Abraham Lincoln helped to free all of the slaves. Sojourner spoke against slavery to anyone who would listen, and she also spoke up for women's right to vote.

Directions: Imagine you are Sojourner Truth. List three reasons you might give to convince others that slavery is wrong.

1. _____

   _____

2. _____

   _____

3. _____

   _____

Now list three reasons why women should have the right to vote.

4. _____

   _____

5. _____

   _____

6. _____

   _____

The Underground Railroad helped many slaves find their way to freedom. It was not actually a railway, but a series of safe places for slaves to hide as they made their way to the north. List three adjectives to describe the type of people who might have helped slaves escape to the North.

7. _____

8. _____

9. _____

Know Your State

Directions: See how much you can find out about your state.

1. In what state do you live? _____

2. What states, if any, border your state? _____

_____

3. What year did your state enter the Union? _____

4. Was your state involved in the Revolutionary War? _____

5. Was your state involved in the Civil War? _____

6. Describe your state's flag.   Draw a sketch of it below. _____

_____

7. Who were the earliest settlers in your state? _____

8. What is the capital of your state? _____

9. In what city do you live, or what is the nearest city to where you live? _____

10. How long have you and your family lived in your state? _____

State Symbols

Directions: Answer the questions below. You may need to look up information about your state.

1. In what state do you live? _____

2. What is your state's flower? _____

3. Draw and color a picture of your state's flower.

4. What is your state's motto? _____

   _____

5. Does your state have a nickname? If so, what is it? _____

   _____

6. Name an important building or famous landmark in your state. _____

   _____

7. Why is this building or landmark well known? _____

   _____
   _____

8. What is your state's bird? _____

9. Draw and color a picture of your state's bird.

Come and Visit

Directions: Imagine you are on the Tourism Board for your city. You have been asked to make a flyer to promote your city and your state. Complete the brochure below to help others learn more about your great area.

Welcome to the Great State of _____
and the beautiful town of _____

Our community is best known for _____

People love to visit here because _____

My home is located at _____

I love my home because _____

My favorite place to go in our state is _____

I like this place because _____

Our state bird is the _____
and it looks like this:

Our state tree is the _____
and it looks like this:

Other interesting facts you should know are _____

My state is simply great because _____

What's in Your Past?

Directions: Answer the questions below. You may need to look up information about your state.

1. Immigrants are people who _____

    _____

2. The first immigrants to your state were most likely from what continent? _____

    _____

3. When did your state gain its statehood? _____

4. Was your state one of the original 13 colonies? _____

5. Name one famous historical figure from your state. _____

    _____

6. Why is this person famous? _____

    _____

7. Draw an outline of your state and write the names of any states that border it.

8. Is there any geographical feature that is important to your state? (For example, a mountain range or a large river, etc.) _____

    _____

9. Were there any Native Americans that were original settlers to your area? If so, what tribes were settled in your state? _____

    _____

    _____

10. How do you think your state received its name? _____

    _____

    _____

    _____

Living Things

Part I

Directions: Read each statement. If the statement about living things is true, write True. If the statement about living things is false, write False.

_____ 1. Living things never change.

_____ 2. All living things must adapt to their environment.

_____ 3. Living things never reproduce.

_____ 4. Living things start small and usually grow larger.

_____ 5. Living things rarely need light or water.

Part II

Directions: Look at the pictures below. Write the numbers 1–4 underneath each picture to place them in the correct sequence.

_____

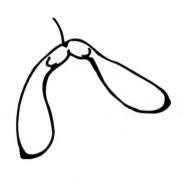

_____

_____

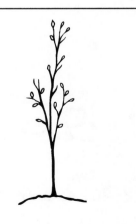

_____

The Importance of Environment

Directions: All living things must adapt to their environments. Read the paragraph below and fill in the correct answers. Use the word bank to help you.

Word Bank				
water	food	weather	desert	adapt
living	protection	sunlight	environment	

A plant's or animal's _____ is everything that is around the plant or animal. All living things must _____ to their environment. For example, a cactus survives the environment of the _____ by storing water for use during long periods of time with no rain.

All living things require liquid _____ to survive. Animals and people need energy from _____ to grow and reproduce. _____ is important to plants because they use it to make food in a process called photosynthesis.

_____ things are also unique because they must have protection against harsh weather conditions. When the _____ gets bad, living things must be ready. People must find _____ during storms. One way to do this is to seek shelter. Plants must also have protection against the weather. Trees and plants are often able to bend with a strong wind rather than break during bad weather.

Parts of a Plant

Part I

Directions: Color the picture below. Then, use the word bank to label the parts of the plant.

Word Bank			
flower	leaf	stem	roots

Part II

Directions: Answer each question.

1. Which part of the plant has the seeds? _____

2. Which part of the plant helps keep the plant straight and upright? _____

3. Which part of the plant helps the plant get water from the ground? _____

4. Which part of the plant that is above ground helps make food for the plant? _____

5. Which part of the plant is attractive to some insects? _____

6. Which part of the plant takes in minerals from the soil? _____

Parts with Purpose

Directions: Write the number of the correct description next to each picture.

1.

6.

2.

7.

3.

8.

4.

9.

5.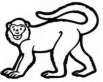

10.

a. This animal's feathers, called down, help keep it warm. _____

b. This animal's long tail keeps insects away from its body. _____

c. This animal's fur blends in perfectly with its wooded environment. _____

d. This animal's speed helps it escape from would-be predators. _____

e. This animal's ability to camouflage itself makes it practically invisible in any environment. _____

f. This animal's sharp teeth are used for protection and to attack. _____

g. This animal's sharp claws are used to hunt prey at night. _____

h. This animal's ability to climb helps it find safety and food. _____

i. This animal's sharp quills keep predators away. _____

j. This animal's strong legs help it jump and attack. _____

Life Cycles

Animals change as they grow, but all animals do not change and grow in the same way. One example of this is the butterfly. The butterfly starts as an egg. From the egg, a caterpillar is born. Eventually the caterpillar forms a casing around itself and becomes a pupa. After about a week, a beautiful butterfly emerges from the pupa.

Directions: Think for a minute about your own life cycle. Draw at least five pictures showing the stages of life you have experienced and/or will experience. Beside each picture, write at least one characteristic that is unique to each stage of development.

Life Stage	Unique Characteristic

Heredity or Not?

Heredity deals with the characteristics an organism inherits from its parents. For example, if you have blue eyes and your parents have blue eyes, this is a trait you have inherited. Some characteristics are not inherited but are learned traits. A person's manners are an example of a learned trait.

Part I

Directions: Read each example. If it is an inherited trait, write the letter *I*. If it is a learned trait, write the letter L.

_____ 1. Big feet

_____ 2. Being able to swim

_____ 3. Naturally curly hair

_____ 4. A good singing voice

_____ 5. Being able to name all fifty states

_____ 6. Being short or tall

_____ 7. A positive attitude

_____ 8. Freckles

_____ 9. Getting good grades in school

_____10. Being polite

Part II

Directions: On the back of this page, draw a picture of yourself. Then list at least four traits about you that are inherited traits rather than learned traits.

1. _____

2. _____

3. _____

4. _____

Not Your Typical Grocery Store

For plants and animals, the world outside is like a grocery store; it's a giant source of food. Some animals eat only plants. These animals are herbivores. Some animals eat only meat. These animals are carnivores. Some animals eat both plants and meat. These animals are omnivores.

Directions: Inside each cart, write h(*herbivore*), c(*carnivore*), or o(*omnivore*) to describe each animal.

Food Chains and Food Webs

All living things need food to get energy. Some living things can make their own food. They are called *producers*. A *consumer* is a living thing that cannot make its own food. Some consumers, called *herbivores*, eat only plants. Other consumers, called *carnivores*, eat only meat. Still others are known as *omnivores* because they eat both plants and meat. There are some living things that break down and consume dead plants and animals. These organisms are called *decomposers*. All of these living and nonliving things create what is known as a *food chain*. A food chain explains how a living thing gets the food it needs for energy. When a food chain links to another food chain, it becomes a *food web*.

Directions: Draw a line to match each statement to its ending.

1. Organisms that can make their own food are   a. ecosystem

2. In a food chain, organisms transfer   b. carnivores

3. Food chains that link to other food chains become   c. food

4. Animals that eat only plants are   d. decomposers

5. Animals that eat only other animals are   e. energy

6. A consumer is an organism that does not make its own   f. producers

7. Organisms that break down dead plants and animals are   g. herbivores

8. All living and nonliving things in an area make up an   h. food web

Something extra: List four animals that are herbivores and four animals that are carnivores.

           Herbivores   Carnivores

_____   _____

_____   _____

_____   _____

_____   _____

Can you think of any animals that are omnivores?

_____

_____

The World Around You

All living organisms need energy. Living things get energy from the food they eat. An animal that eats only plants for its energy is called an herbivore, an animal that eats only meat for its energy is called a carnivore, and an animal that eats both plants and meat for its energy is called an omnivore. Animals live in habitats where their energy needs can be met.

A food chain shows how living organisms are connected. For example, in a food chain grass would be eaten by a rabbit, and then the rabbit would be eaten by a fox. Each part of the chain is needed to supply energy to the next living organism. Organisms called decomposers break down any leftover food, the nutrients enter the soil to feed plants, and the cycle starts all over again.

Directions: Read each question, and then circle the correct answer.

1. All living organisms need

   a. grass   b. energy

2. Nutrients are recycled back to the earth by

   a. decomposers   b. photosynthesis

3. An organism's home might also be called its

   a. life cycle   b. habitat

4. An animal that eats only plants is called

   a. hungry   b. an herbivore

5. An animal that eats only meat is called

   a. a carnivore   b. an omnivore

6. An organism that eats both plants and animals is called

   a. an omnivore   b. a producer

7. In the food chain a lion would most likely eat

   a. plants   b. animals

8. A food chain shows how living organisms are

   a. connected   b. decompose

Pyramids...Not Just for Egypt

Directions: Energy pyramids are diagrams that show how energy moves through an ecosystem.

Example:

Look at the energy pyramids below and decide what might go in each missing section. Draw a picture and write the name of the plant or animal.

1.   2.   3.   4.

       5.   6.   7.

You and Your Food

Just as other organisms get their energy from a food chain or web, so do humans.

Directions: Think about your eating habits. Write down everything you ate for breakfast, lunch, dinner, and any snacks. Then answer the questions below.

Breakfast: _____

_____

_____

Lunch: _____

_____

_____

Dinner: _____

_____

_____

Snacks: _____

_____

_____

1. Look over your menu. Are your eating habits more like a herbivore, carnivore, or an omnivore?

_____

_____

_____

2. Choose one item from your menu and create an energy pyramid with you at the top of the pyramid.

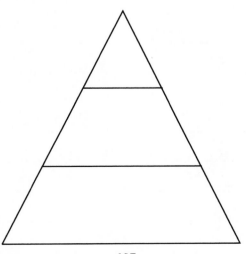

We're All in This Together

Humans make some of the most positive and negative changes affecting the Earth and its ecosystems.

Directions: Color the picture of our world. Then, list five ways people can cause negative changes to the world's ecosystems and five ways people can cause positive changes to the world's ecosystems.

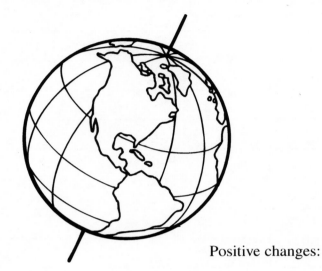

Negative changes: Positive changes:

1. _____   1. _____

    _____   _____

    _____   _____

2. _____   2. _____

    _____   _____

    _____   _____

    _____   _____

3. _____   3. _____

    _____   _____

4. _____   4. _____

    _____   _____

    _____   _____

5. _____   5. _____

    _____   _____

    _____   _____

Rocks Can Be Useful

Rocks are all around us. Although rock is seen in many places, it is not a living organism. However, organisms that were once living can sometimes be found in rocks. These organisms of the past are known as fossils. Because rocks are so hard and durable, they help preserve things from the past so that we can view them today.

Rock is used all over the world. For example, crushed rock is made into gravel. People often use gravel for their driveways. Crushed rock is also used to make cement. Sometimes people use rocks to help them build things such as walls, or they may even use rocks for decoration.

Directions: Make a *T* by each statement that is true and an *F* by each statement that is false.

_____ 1. Rocks can tell us about the past.

_____ 2. Gravel is a form of crushed rock.

_____ 3. Cement is made from crushed rock.

_____ 4. Rocks are living organisms.

_____ 5. Fossils can be found in rocks.

_____ 6. People can use rocks to help them build things

_____ 7. People can use rocks to form pieces of art.

_____ 8. Rocks need water to survive.

Just for fun: Can you name a famous American landmark that is made from rock?

Rocks and Minerals

Not everything on our earth is a plant or an animal. The Earth is also made up of many other things including *minerals* and *rocks*. Minerals are nonliving substances occurring in nature. Minerals combine with each other to make up rocks.

There are three main types of rocks: igneous, sedimentary, and metamorphic. Igneous rocks are formed when hot, molten rock cools and then becomes a solid. Sedimentary rock is formed from sand, mud, or pebbles that pile up on the bottom of rivers, lakes, etc. Metamorphic rocks are formed when existing igneous or sedimentary rock is changed because of heat or pressure from the Earth.

Directions: Color only the rocks that have statements that are true. Place an X on the rocks that have statements that are not true.

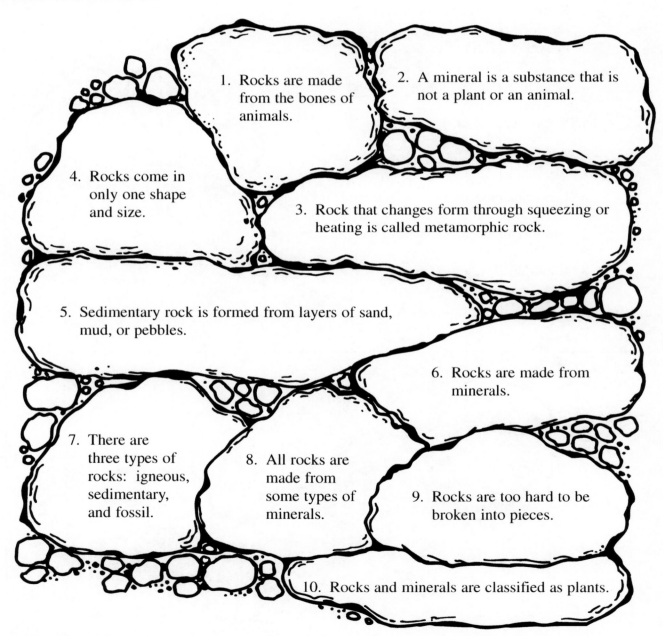

1. Rocks are made from the bones of animals.

2. A mineral is a substance that is not a plant or an animal.

4. Rocks come in only one shape and size.

3. Rock that changes form through squeezing or heating is called metamorphic rock.

5. Sedimentary rock is formed from layers of sand, mud, or pebbles.

6. Rocks are made from minerals.

7. There are three types of rocks: igneous, sedimentary, and fossil.

8. All rocks are made from some types of minerals.

9. Rocks are too hard to be broken into pieces.

10. Rocks and minerals are classified as plants.

Here's the Dirt

Directions: Look at the picture below. Draw at least five things that can grow in the soil. Be sure to color your picture when you are finished.

List at least 3 things your plants would need to help them grow.

1. _____

2. _____

3. _____

Long, Long Ago

The imprint or remains of something in the earth that lived long, long ago is called a fossil.

Part I

Directions: Draw a line and match each fossil to its original owner.

1.   a. a dragonfly

2.   b. a dinosaur

3.   c. a fish

4.   d. a footprint

5.   e. a leaf

Part II

Directions: Color the fossils you find.

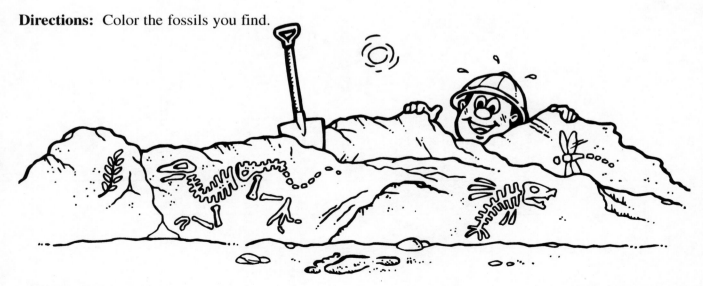

Finding Out More about Fossils

Fossils are imprints found on the Earth that tell about things from the past. Because they are discoveries from the past, scientists use fossils today to study how the world has changed. Today's fossil scientists, called paleontologists, are always discovering something new about the world by studying fossils. Fossils are unique not only because they give information about the past but because they are found in so many shapes, sizes, and places. Some fossils have even been found in the hardened amber that comes from trees. Still other fossils are found in the layers of the Earth's rocks and soil. Fossils are indeed a map to the past.

Directions: Color the fossils that have statements that are true.

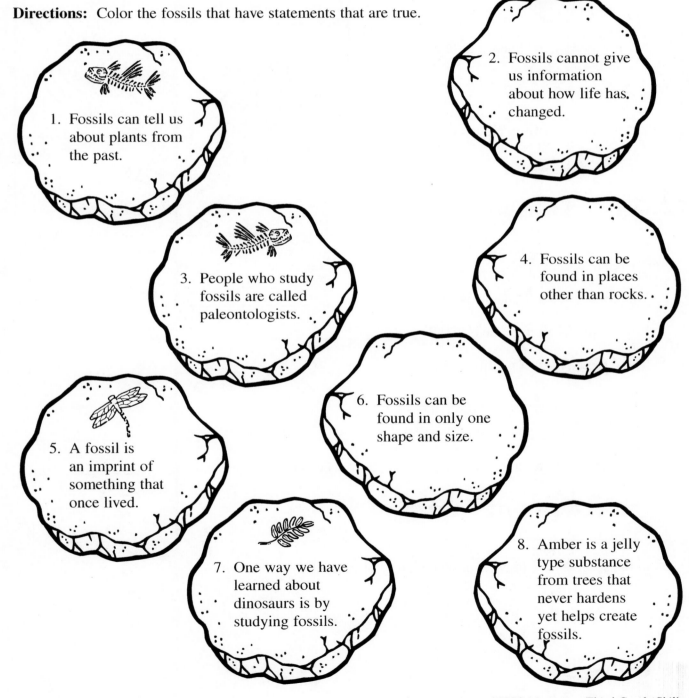

1. Fossils can tell us about plants from the past.

2. Fossils cannot give us information about how life has changed.

3. People who study fossils are called paleontologists.

4. Fossils can be found in places other than rocks.

5. A fossil is an imprint of something that once lived.

6. Fossils can be found in only one shape and size.

7. One way we have learned about dinosaurs is by studying fossils.

8. Amber is a jelly type substance from trees that never hardens yet helps create fossils.

Water, Water Everywhere!

Directions: We all know we need water to survive. Water on earth moves in a continuous cycle from the earth to the sky and back again. Look at the diagram below, and then fill in the blanks.

1. _____ is
   when water changes from liquid to vapor.

2. _____ is
   when water vapor changes to liquid.

3. _____ is
   when water falls from clouds to the earth.

4. _____ is
   when water pools in lakes, seas, and oceans.

5. There are a total of _____ steps in the water cycle.

6. Water that rises into the air is called _____

7. What happens after condensation? _____

8. Name three types of precipitation._____

   _____

   _____

9. List at least two reasons that the water cycle is necessary to the earth. _____

   _____

   _____

10. In the space below draw your own picture of the water cycle.

Find that Hidden Word

Directions: Search across, down, and diagonally to find the words hidden in the word search. Use the word bank to help you in your search.

Word Bank

condensation	precipitation	evaporation	sun
rain	sleet	snow	rivers
oceans	water	lakes	temperature

```
T N F P S E R T T Y R S N G E
E U E U E I E R E V O O V B A
M Y N W V V T M I E I P M H E
P F M E U Z A Q U T L D G L F
E E R T D H W P A A Q S C S S
R S H B L R R T O L Y Y L N R
A R Q L R D I M O R C K Q O A
T A Y J T P H N C N A H R W K
U Q C U I K T R V R F T Q C J
R R W C P L A K E S Y V I Y Z
E Z E C O N D E N S A T I O N
I R U S I Q A R S N A E C O N
P R P R O Q K M A Q C I E Q C
G S E J C I A T L I C U U S L
M Q N K Q E E W I L N P W Q J
```

Night and Day

Part I

Directions: Answer each question below.

List three things you normally do when it is daylight.

1. _____

2. _____

3. _____

List three things you normally do when it is dark.

4. _____

5. _____

6. _____

Part II

Directions: Read the short paragraph and then answer the questions.

Night and day are caused by the Earth's rotation on its axis. Where the Earth is turned away from the sun, it is night. Where the Earth is turned towards the sun, it is day. It takes twenty-four hours for the Earth to make a complete rotation. This twenty-four hour rotation makes one day.

7. How long does it take for the earth to make a complete rotation? _____

8. What causes the Earth to have night and day? _____

_____

9. When it is day, part of the Earth is turned towards the _____ .

10. When it is night, part of the Earth is turned _____ from the sun.

The Sun and the Moon

You know that night and day are caused by the Earth's rotation on its axis. As the Earth turns, the part of the Earth facing the sun has day. The part of the Earth not facing the sun has night. Because of the sun and the moon and the rotation of the Earth, we have light and dark or day and night. This rotation of the Earth helps you decide when to do many of your daily activities.

Directions: Look at each picture below. If the event usually occurs in the day, draw a sun below the picture. If the event usually occurs at night, draw a moon below the picture.

1.

5.

2.

6.

3.

7.

4.

8.

Best Choice

Directions: Read the information and then read each question. Circle the answer that is the best choice.

Our planet Earth is part of a solar system that is made up of the sun and all the objects that orbit the sun. The planets that are in our solar system are commonly divided into two groups. These groups are known as the inner planets and the outer planets. The inner planets are the planets that are closest to the sun. The outer planets are the planets that are not as close to the sun. Earth is considered an inner planet. The Earth rotates or spins on its axis. It takes the earth twenty-four hours, or one day, to complete a rotation.

The moon is also part of our solar system. The moon goes through different phases depending on the amount of light it gets from the sun. Although the shape of the moon does not really change, the moon appears to change in shape as it goes through its four phases.

1. Earth makes a complete rotation in

    a. 24 hours

    b. 1 week

2. The solar system is made up of the sun and all of the objects that

    a. orbit the sun

    b. are in outer space

3. Earth rotates or spins on its

    a. northern side

    b. axis

4. The moon goes through

    a. two phases

    b. four phases

5. The planets are divided into two groups: the inner planets and

    a. the outer planets

    b. the larger planets

The Man in the Moon

Just as the Earth orbits the sun, the moon orbits the Earth. Because of this orbit, the moon appears to change shapes. The apparent changes of the moon are called its phases. As you gaze at the moon you may even see what looks like a face, otherwise known as the Man in the Moon. The face is, in fact, nothing more than craters on the moon's surface.

Part I

Directions: Look at the pictures of the moon. Use the word bank to help you label the different phases of the moon.

Word Bank			
Last quarter moon	First quarter moon	New moon	Full moon

_____   _____   _____   _____

Part II

Directions: Imagine that there really is a man in the moon. Write a short explanation telling who he is and how he got there. Explain why he stays on the moon. Then, on the back of this sheet, draw your own picture of the man in the moon.

_____

_____

_____

_____

_____

_____

_____

What's Out There?

Part I

Directions: Label and color each planet in our solar system. Use the word bank if you need help.

Word Bank
Mercury   Venus   Earth   Mars   Jupiter   Saturn   Uranus   Neptune   Pluto

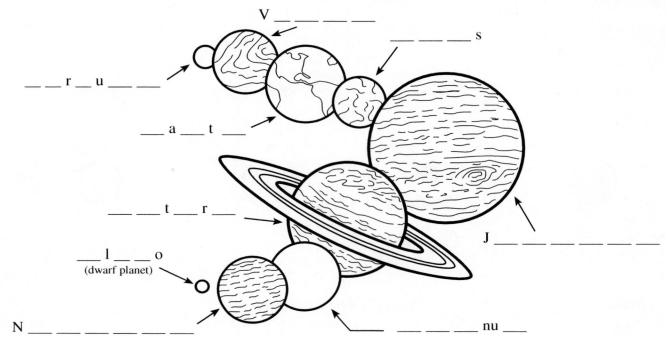

V _ _ _ _ _

_ _ _ s

_ _ r _ u _ _ _

_ _ a _ t _ _

_ _ _ t _ r _ _

J _ _ _ _ _ _ _

_ _ l _ _ o
(dwarf planet)

N _ _ _ _ _ _ _

_ _ _ _ nu _

Part II

Directions: If you could create a new planet for our solar system, what would you name it? What would it look like? Where would you place it among the planets? Would your planet have anyone living on it?

Write about your new planet, and then draw a picture of your new planet. Use your own piece of paper or the back of this one if you need more space.

_____

_____

_____

_____

_____

_____

The Inner Planets

Part I

Directions: Below are the four inner planets drawn in order from the sun. Color each planet.

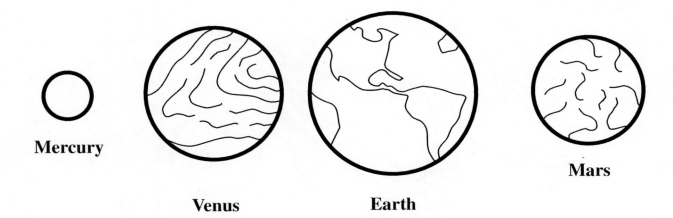

Mercury

Venus   Earth   Mars

Part II

Directions: Answer each question about the four inner planets.

1. _____ is one of the inner planets, and it is closest to the sun.

2. _____ is the inner planet that was named after a female goddess. It is the second closest planet to the sun.

3. Our planet, _____ , is also one of the inner planets. It is sometimes called "the third rock from the sun".

4. The inner planet known as the red planet is _____ . It is the last of the inner planets.

5. Planet Earth gets its light from the _____ .

6. On what inner planet do you live? _____

The Outer Planets

Part I

Directions: Below are the four outer planets (and dwarf planet Pluto) drawn in order from the sun and the inner planets. Color each planet.

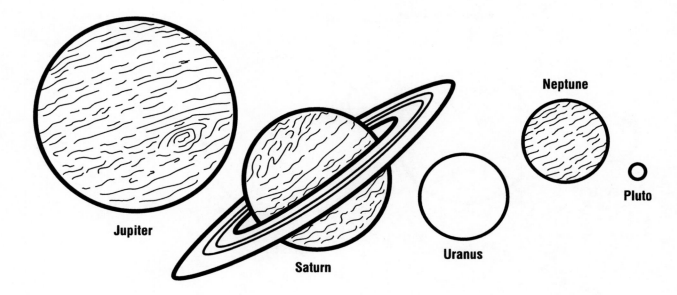

Part II

Directions: Use the pictures above to help you match each planet to its correct answer.

1. Neptune   a. This planet is the third of the outer planets.

2. Jupiter   b. There is little known about this small, cold space object that is so far from the sun.

3. Saturn   c. This planet is the largest planet in our solar system.

4. Pluto   d. This planet is known for the rings that circle it.

5. Uranus   e. This planet is the fourth outer planet and was named after the god of the sea in mythology.

Gravity – the Force that's Really with You

Gravity is an invisible force that pulls objects towards the Earth. The further away an object is the less gravity acts as a force on the object. For example, the moon is held in orbit by Earth's gravitational pull but because the moon is so far away, gravity does not pull the moon into the Earth. However, if you went outside and picked up a ball and then dropped it, the ball would immediately fall to the ground. This is an example of gravity in action.

Directions: Imagine you wake up one morning and you and everything in your bedroom are floating off the ground. For one day only there is no gravity on the Earth. How would your day be different? What would be hard to do? What would be easier to do? Write a short story about your day without gravity.

_____

_____

_____

_____

_____

_____

_____

_____

_____

_____

_____

Going to the Races

Motion and speed are terms we use when talking about how an object moves.

Motion: An object is in motion if it is changing position.

Speed: Speed is a measure of an object's rate of motion. Speed is usually measured by the time it takes for an object to travel a certain distance. If an object moves faster, its speed increases. If an object slows down, its speed decreases.

Directions: Read a statement on each can about motion and speed. If the statement is a fact, color the race car. If the statement is not a fact, do nothing to the race car.

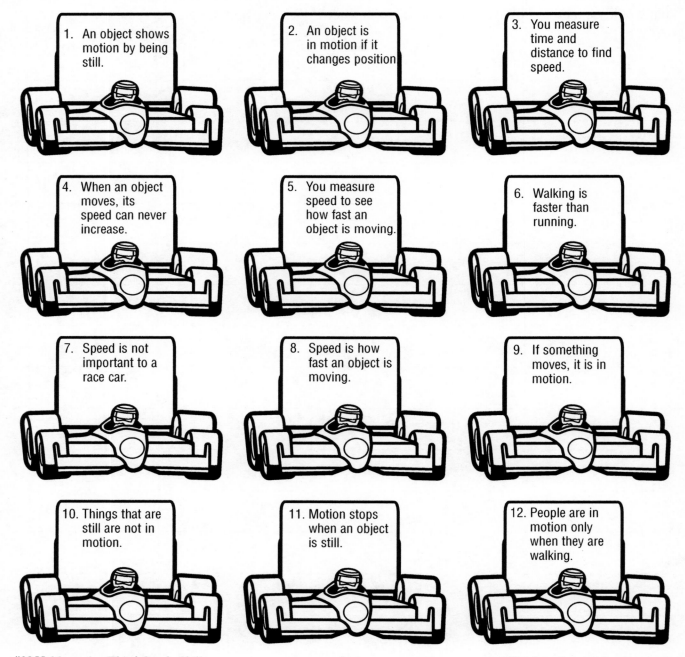

Push and Pull

Pushes and pulls are forces. A force is able to change the motion of an object. Of course, the heavier an object is the more force it takes to move that object.

Directions: Look at each picture. Write "push" if you would push the object to move it. Write "pull" if you would pull the object to move it.

1. _____

2. _____

3. _____

4. _____

5. _____

6. _____

7. _____

8. _____

9. _____

10. _____

10. _____

11. _____

Something Extra: Try to think of something you both push and pull. For example, you both push and pull a vacuum cleaner. See how many objects you can list.

_____

_____

_____

_____

_____

_____

_____

Green Light, Red Light

Motion can be seen when a car approaches a stop light. If the light is green, the driver pushes the gas pedal and the force of the engine keeps the car moving. Force can change the direction and speed of an object, like when a bat hits a baseball.

If the light turns red, the driver pushes the brakes, which use friction to slow the car down. Friction is produced when two materials rub against each other and causes an object in motion to slow down or stop. Friction can also cause heat—try rubbing your hands together quickly. Can you feel the heat caused by friction?

Directions: Circle the best answer.

1. _____ happens when an object rubs against another object.

   a. friction

   b. motion

2. Friction can cause an object to _____

   a. move faster

   b. slow down or stop

3. A _____ can change the motion of an object.

   a. distance

   b. force

4. A force can cause an object in motion to _____

   a. speed up

   b. be heavier

5. Friction can create _____

   a. distance

   b. heat

Magnetic Attraction

A magnet is a special object that can attract certain metals like iron or steel. This magnetic attraction or pull is called magnetic force. Some metals like copper or aluminum are not attracted to magnets – there would be no push or pull if a magnet was placed near one of these metals. Magnets have both positive and negative poles. These poles can cause magnets to push or pull another magnet.

Part I

Directions: Look at each object below. If the object could be attracted to a magnet, circle it. If there would be no attraction or motion, place an X on the object.

1.

2.

3.

4.

5.

6.

7.

8.

9.

10.

11

12.

13.

14.

Crossword Fun

Directions: Complete the crossword puzzle by answering each question.

Word Bank	
motion	push
stopped	forces
gravity	position
pull	speed

Across

3. If an object changes its _____, then it is in motion.

5. Pushes and pulls are examples of _____.

6. An example of a force used to move a toy wagon would be a _____.

7. How fast or slow an object is moving is the object's _____.

Down

1. Things fall to Earth because of _____.

2. Force is what puts an object in _____.

3. An example of a force used to move a baby stroller would be a _____.

4. When an object is no longer in motion, the object has _____.

Name that Substance

 A *solid* has definite shape, mass, and volume. An example is an apple you can eat.

 A *liquid* has no definite shape, but it does have mass and volume. An example is orange juice you can drink.

 A *gas* has no definite shape, mass, or volume. An example is steam from a boiling pot.

Directions: Label each substance as a solid, liquid, or gas.

Substance   Form

1. water   _____

2. oxygen   _____

3. wood   _____

4. juice   _____

5. helium   _____

6. concrete   _____

7. ice   _____

8. lemonade   _____

9. nitrogen   _____

10. milk   _____

11. tea   _____

12. metal   _____

13. coffee   _____

14. hydrogen   _____

15. steel   _____

Solid, Liquid, and Gas

Part I

Matter can be classified as a solid, a liquid, or a gas. List five examples of each of the different states of matter.

	Solid	**Liquid**	**Gas**
Example:	wood	water	hydrogen

Solid	Liquid	Gas
1. _____	1. _____	1. _____
2. _____	2. _____	2. _____
3. _____	3. _____	3. _____
4. _____	4. _____	4. _____
5. _____	5. _____	5. _____

Part II

Directions: In the space below draw and label examples of matter in the state of a solid and matter in the state of a liquid. Do not use any of the examples you listed above.

Solid	Liquid

More or Less

Mass is the amount of matter in an object. Matter is made up of particles. When the particles are tightly packed the object has more mass. Therefore, the more mass an object has, the more the object will weigh.

Directions: Circle the object that has more mass.

1.

2.

3.

4.

5.

6.

7.

8.

9.

10.

11.

12.

13.

14.

15.

16.

17.

18.

19.

20.

What's the Matter?

Directions: Answer each question below. Use the word bank if you need help.

Word Bank				
properties	mass	size	color	gas
particles	weight	solid	liquid	shape

1. Matter can be described by its characteristics or _____ .

2. Three characteristics of matter are _____ , _____, and_____.

3. Oxygen is an example of matter that is a _____.

4. Water is an example of matter that is a _____.

5. Ice is an example of matter that is a _____.

6. _____ is the amount of matter in an object.

7. The more mass an object has, the more _____ an object has on Earth.

8. Matter is made up of _____; the more tightly packed they are, the more an object weighs.

Find That Word!

Directions: Find the words hidden in the word search. Words can be hidden horizontally, vertically, or diagonally.

M	V	T	S	U	G	W	F	W	Z	J	S	S	H	S
K	A	H	E	Y	R	E	T	A	W	O	E	I	N	Z
T	F	T	I	W	O	I	M	A	L	L	E	P	C	X
Y	O	K	T	Z	E	G	Q	I	C	M	G	A	S	E
F	P	Q	R	E	U	H	D	I	K	N	A	Q	T	X
B	B	H	E	U	R	T	T	B	J	U	D	E	K	H
M	J	R	P	N	N	R	S	C	D	P	M	Z	T	N
N	P	I	O	U	A	F	S	J	R	B	T	Y	Q	S
I	T	U	R	P	Y	D	A	C	M	W	R	Y	Y	Q
X	V	W	P	L	F	F	M	F	I	B	C	M	E	S
F	B	K	V	R	L	G	Q	M	S	N	R	U	J	H
L	I	Q	U	I	D	I	C	T	L	O	A	B	J	N
F	G	V	E	J	T	T	K	Y	F	F	U	E	A	E
Q	S	P	B	I	S	P	U	N	L	R	S	I	Q	S
Y	U	B	E	Q	Q	S	W	X	B	C	B	O	V	W

solid	matter	weight	ice
gas	properties	particles	steam
liquid	mass	water	form

Answer Key

Page 34

Answers will vary

Page 35

1. C
3. C
4. C
6. C
8. C
10. C

Page 36

Part I

1. his
2. they
3. her
4. they
5. her

Part II

he, she, it, they, you, me, I, us, we

Page 37

he—Jack

she—Mandy

it—sunshine

they— Brett, Sadie, and Gage

we—Joan and I

Page 38

Answers will vary

Page 39

1. a puppy
2. a tree
3. a baseball glove
4. a computer
5. a cow

6. a piano
7. a television
8. a cupcake
9. a flower
10. a necklace

Page 40

1. apples
2. shirts
3. coats
4. computers
5. movies
6. stars
7. cars
8. trees
9. flowers
10. shoes

Page 41

Answers will vary

Page 42

1. geese
2. stories
3. men
4. oxen
5. leaves
6. berries
7. ladies
8. deer
9. pennies
10. women

Page 43

Common nouns

1. pizza, supper
2. friend, person

3. cake
4. game
5. sisters
6. bus, students, school
7. teacher, apple
8. teacher, pencil
9. snake, tree
10. day

Proper nouns

1. Jennifer, Fridays
2. (none)
3. Joe
4. Mom, Dad
5. Chloe, Kayla Beth
6. (none)
7. Ella
8. Gage
9. Sally
10. Tuesday

Page 44

Answers will vary

Page 45

Answers will vary

Page 46

Actions verbs: sit, skip, ran, sing, start, stop, find, tease, laugh, give

Page 47

Present tense (these should be circled)

1. finish
2. carry
3. clean
4. paint

Answer Key *(cont.)*

5. walk
6. laugh
7. lift
8. grin
9. talk
10. wrap
11. pick

Page 48

Answers will vary

Page 49

Answers will vary

Page 50

Answers will vary

Page 51

How many (yellow)

4. some
6. few
8. several

Which ones (blue)

1. these
3. My

What kind (orange)

2. red
3. favorite, best
4. green
5. fresh
7. shriveled
9. delicious
10. wonderful

Page 52

1. early, late
2. outside, inside
3. first, last

4. tomorrow
5. carefully

6–10. Answers will vary

Page 53

1. quickly
2. yesterday
3. now
4. gladly
5. late
6. everywhere
7. slowly
8. today
9. upstairs
10. quietly

Page 54

Answers will vary

Page 55

Part I

Answers will vary

Part II

6. New York
7. Washington, D.C.
8. Pennsylvania
9. San Francisco

Page 56

Part I

Arrowhead

Hill, Tennessee

February

Dear

Sincerely

Part II

Answers will vary

Page 57

Answers will vary

Page 58

1. Mr. Smith
2. Kentucky
3. Captain Brown
4. United States of America
5. Europe
6. Atlantic Ocean
7. Oak Street
8. Valentine's Day
9. Monday
10. January
11. Dear Jason,
12. Ashland City
13. Saturday
14. St. Patrick's Day
15. Nashville

Page 59

Capt.

Mrs.

St.

Dr.

Sept.

Tues.

J.C.

F.B.I.

Ms.

Fri.

Page 60

Answers will vary

Answer Key (cont.)

Page 61

1. B
2. A
3. B
4. B
5. A
6. B
7 B
8. B
9. A
10. A

Page 62

San Jose, California

October 26, 2005

Dear Sandra,

Your friend,

Page 63

1. d
2. j
3. f
4. g
5. h
6. i
7. c
8. a
9. b
10. e

Page 64

1. do not
2. is not
3. can not
4. are not
5. does not
6. have not
7. Michele is
8. will not
9. He is
10. did not

Page 65

1. Emily's candy
2. Chien's DVD
3. Tyrese's backpack
4. Rafael's camera
5. Keysha's necklace
6. Elissa's game
7. Sharon's puzzle
8. Samuel's shoes
9. Aina's book
10. Brody's bike

Page 66

1. student's lunch
2. mother's purse
3. Bailey's toy
4. child's shoe
5. pirate's treasure
6. bear's fur
7. tree's leaves
8. flower's petals
9. library's books
10. shark's teeth

Page 67

Answers will vary

Page 68

1. "I can't wait for summer vacation," Ted said.
2. "I can't wait either," Addison agreed.
3. "Where are you going on vacation?" Ted asked.
4. "We're going to Hawaii," Addison said.
5. "That sounds very nice," Ted replied.
6. "Where are you going?" Addison asked.
7. Ted replied, "Well, it's not exactly Hawaii, but there is water there."
8. "Well, where is it?" Addison asked again.
9. "I'm going to spend my vacation working at my Uncle Bob's carwash," Ted finally told her.
10. "I guess you're right. There will be plenty of water," Addison said with a smile.

Page 69

Sentences with personification:

2, 3, 5, 7, 8

Page 70

Answers will vary

Page 71

Answers will vary

Page 72

Answers will vary

Page 73

Metaphors:

chocolate is a dream

it is gold for the tongue

chocolate is definitely heaven

chocolate is a cartoon character

Page 74

Answer Key (cont.)

Part I

Answers will vary

Part II

5. H   7. H

6. X   8. X

Page 75

Answers will vary

Page 76

Answers will vary

Page 77

1. E
2. A
3. B
4. C
5. D

6–10 Answers will vary

Page 78

Answers will vary

Page 79

1. 8
2. 8
3. 10
4. 8
5. 7
6. 9
7. 9
8. 9
9. 6
10. 6
11. 6
12. 10
13. 8
14. 7

15. 8

Page 80

1. 11
2. 15
3. 10
4. 7
5. 11
6. 11
7. 4
8. 8
9. 17
10. 13

Page 81

1. D
2. A
3. B
4. D
5. B

Page 82

1. 3
2. 4
3. 5
4. 0
5. 0
6. 8
7. 10
8. 9
9. 9
10. 4

Page 83

1. 40
2. 50
3. 101
4. 32

5. 32
6. 40
7. 81
8. 100
9. 80
10. 71
11. 71
12. 90
13. 31
14. 82
15. 42
16. 32
17. 22
18. 31
19. 64
20. 36
21. 83

Page 84

1. 517
2. 350
3. 781
4. 230
5. 902
6. 441
7. 861
8. 770
9. 781
10. 869 pennies
11. 349 days
12. 922 cards

Answer Key (cont.)

Page 85
1. 67
2. 99
3. 111
4. 87
5. 95
6. 110
7. 90
8. 107
9. 116
10. 48
11. 102
12. 90
13. 75
14. 43
15. 114
16. 99
17. 96
18. 110
19. 95

Page 86
1. 21.34
2. 28.90
3. 99.22
4. 22.04
5. 29.6
6. 16.8
7. 74.6
8. 8.1
9. 11.09
10. 11.20
11. 40.5
12. 34.00
13. 13.42
14. 47.89
15. 99.23
16. 33.33
17. 96.65
18. 111.10

Page 87
1. 3
2. 5
3. 7
4. 1
5. 1
6. 2
7. 2
8. 0
9. 4
10. 3
11. 6
12. 3
13. 3
14. 2
15. 4
16. 3
17. 3
18. 0
19. 3
20. 5

Page 88
1. 74
2. 11
3. 57
4. 47
5. 65
6. 7
7. 69
8. 28
9. 66
10. 50
11. 13
12. 1
13. 2
14. 10
15. 10
16–19 Answers will vary

Page 89
1. 28
2. 9
3. 20
4. 43
5. 57
6. 500
7. 356
8. 42
9. 50
10. 12
11. 33
12. 55
13. 31
14. 31
15. 58
16. 27
17. 45
18. 15
19. 10
20. 33
21. 10

Page 90

Answer Key *(cont.)*

1. 619
2. 111
3. 289
4. 23
5. 110
6. 218
7. 10
8. 90
9. 348
10. 369
11. 0
12. 591
13. 728
14. 10
15. 61

Page 91

1. 212
2. 432
3. 427
4. 440
5. 191
6. 120
7. 362
8. 239
9. 214
10. 355
11. 65
12. 93
13. 73
14. 10
15. 35
16. 346
17. 203

18. 173
19. 100
20. 100
21. 12
22. 74
23. 386
24. 307

Page 92

1. 15 students
2. 26 turtles
3. 250 candy bars
4. 31 lemonade products
5. 767 acorns

Page 93

1. $40.55
2. $12.09
3. $21.65
4. $18.01
5. $43.39
6. $47.44
7. $ 2.00
8. $ 6.20
9. $ 9.10
10. $80.00
11. $60.20
12. $10.20
13. $1.48
114.1 $7.12

Where will you never find
money? Growing on trees!

Page 94

1. 16
2. 25
3. 18

4. 12
5. 16
6. 7
7. 9
8. 28

Page 95

1. 3
2. 4
3. 6
4. 9
5. 21
6. 16
7. 6
8. 10
9. 18
10. 24

Page 96

1. 16
2. 25
3. 36
4. 0
5. 0
6. 0
7. 12
8. 15
9. 18
10. 28
11. 35
12. 42
13. 40
14. 50
15. 60
16. 32

Answer Key (cont.)

17. 40
18. 48
19. 8
20. 10
21. 12
22. 20
23. 25
24. 30
25. 36
26. 45
27. 54
28. 48
29. 60
30. 72

Page 97

1. 7
2. 56
3. 21
4. 54
5. 0
6. 42
7. 24
8. 14
9. 72
10. 28
11. 18
12. 56
13. 27
14. 35
15. 48
16. 90
17. 96
18. 99

19. 64
20. 49

Page 98

1. 100
2. 66
3. 60
4. 40
5. 88
6. 84
7. 20
8. 33
9. 144
10. 110
11. 11
12. 48
13. 60
14. 66
15. 24
16. 121
17. 100
18. 12

Page 99

1. 4
2. 120
3. 28
4. 16
5. 27
6. 63
7. 0
8. 45
9. 72
10. 132
11. 21

12. 18
13. 30
14. 16
15. 81

Page 100

Students should circle two equal groups and leave remainders for each problem.

Page 101

1. 9
2. 5
3. 12
4. 4
5. 8
6. 10
7. 3
8. 7
9. 11
10. 3
11. 4
12. 8
13. 6
14. 7
15. 5
16. 2
17. 9
18. 11
19. 2
20. 3
21. 3
22. 2
23. 2
24. 2

Page 102

Answer Key (cont.)

1. X
2. Color
3. Color
4. X
5. Color
6. Color
7. X
8. Color
9. Color
10. X
11. Color
12. X
13. Color
14. Color
15. X

Page 103

1. 3
2. 2
3. 9
4. 5
5. 7
6. 12
7. 1
8. 4
9. 11
10. 6
11. 8

You are smart!

Page 104

1. 3
2. 2
3. 10
4. 11

5. 4
6. 3
7. 5
8. 7
9. 5
10. 2
11. 2
12. 10
13. 8
14. 7

Page 105

1. 9, 27
2. 3, 12
3. 3, 18
4. 5, 10
5. 8, 88
6. 5, 45
7. 7, 7
8. 7, 28
9. 12, 36
10. 6, 60
11. 11, 44
12. 4, 24
13. 10, 50
14. 7, 56
15. 7, 14
16. 12, 48

Page 106

1. c
2. b
3. a
4. c
5. d

6. a
7. a
8. c

Page 107

1. 5
2. 6
3. 10
4. 5
5. 20
6. 20
7. 10
8. 10
9. 5
10. 3
11. 10
12. 8
13. 700
14. 10
15. 10
16. 80
17. 5
18. 2
19. 40
20. 10

Page 108

1. 2, 20, 200, 2000
2. 3, 30, 300, 3000
3. 4, 40, 400, 4000
4. 6, 60, 600, 6000
5. 5, 50, 500, 5000
6. 3, 30, 300, 3000
7. 1, 10, 100, 1000
8. 4, 40, 400, 4000

Answer Key (cont.)

9. 2, 20, 200, 2000
10. 2, 20, 200, 2000

Page 109
1. 36 r1
2. 18 r3
3. 12 r1
4. 10 r8
5. 13 r2
6. 10 r2
7. 19 r3
8. 28 r1
9. 14 r1
10. 3 r3
11. 27 r1
12. 12 r1
13. 18 r1
14. 2 r3
15. 24 r1
16. 2 r3
17. 12 r2
18. 14 r4
19. 12 r1
20. 31 r7
21. 44 pieces, yes

Page 110
1. b
2. a
3. c
4. e
5. f
6. d
7.–10. Drawings will vary

Page 111
1. 3/10

2. 3/6
3. 1/6
4. 7/8
5. 5/8
6. 2/3
7. 4/7
8. 1/2

Page 112

Answers will vary

Page 113
1. 5/5
2. 5/8
3. 2/3
4. 5/6
5. 4/4
6. 7/10
7. 3/8
8. 3/6
9. 4/10
10. 1/4
11. 1/3
12. 2/9
13. 3/3
14. 1/6

Page 114
1. 0
2. 4/4
3. 6/8
4. 3/8
5. 2/7
6. 5/5
7. 3/3
8. 5/12
9. 5/6

10. 6/8
11. 2/8
12. 4/6
13. 1/3
14. 6/8
15. 10/10
16. 9/12
17. 6/9
18. 2/6

Page 115
1. 1/2
2. 1/2
3. 1/2
4. 1/2
5. 1/2

Page 116
1. c
2. b
3. a
4. c

Page 117
1. 16 cents
2. 95 cents
3. 83 cents
4. 35 cents
5. 50 cents
6. 70 cents
7. 87 cents
8. 80 cents
9. 75 cents

Page 118
1. $3.40, Yes
2. $4.75

Answer Key (cont.)

3. 10 cents

4. 32 cents

Page 119

1. $10.05

2. $11.20

3. 98 cents

4. $4.80

5. $3.30

6. $1.13

7. $8.00

8. 39 cents

9. 86 cents

10. $2.80

Page 120

1. 10, 12, 14

2. Z, Y, Z

3. circle, triangle, square

4. 12, 10, 8

5. 600, 700, 800

6. 2 squares, 2 triangles, 2 circles

7. 2 stars, 4 stars, 2 stars

8. 34, 35, 36

9. 947, 937, 927

10. a dime, a nickel, a quarter

11. Y, Z, X

12. 32, 64, 128

13. CC, D, DD

Page 121

Part I

1. j

2. a

3. h

4. i

5. g

6. b

7. c

8. e

9. f

10. d

Part II

11. 13x13, 14x14, 15x15

12. JKL, MNO, PQR

13. 4444, 55555, 666666

14. 70, 85, 100

15. 1/7, 1/8, 1/9

Page 122

1. a

2. b

3. a

4. c

5. a

6. b

Page 123

1. 5 inches

2. 6 inches

3. 4 inches

4. 6 inches

5. 3 inches

Page 124

1. 7cm

2. 1dm

3. 5cm

Page 125

1. b

2. a

3. b

4. a

5. b

6. a

7. b

8. a

9. a

10. a

Page 126

1. b

2. a

3. a

4. b

5. a

6. b

7. a

8. b

Page 127

Part I

1. >

2. <

3. <

4. >

5. <

6. <

Part II

7. a

8. b

9. a

10. b

Answer Key *(cont.)*

11. a

12. b

13. a

14. a

15. a

16. a

Page 128

1. 40° F

2. 85° F

3. 10° F

4. 20° F

5. 50° F

6. 90° F

7. 15° F

8. 30° F

9. 75° F

10. 30° F

11. 98° F

12. 40° F

13. 70° F

Page 129

1. 8 inches

2. 9 inches

3. 12 inches

4. 4 inches

5. 18 inches

Page 130

1. 8 square units

2. 10 square units

3. 6 square units

4. 5 square units

5. 3 square units

6. 4 square units

Page 131

Answers will vary

Page 132

1. cone

2. cube

3. rectangular prism

4. rectangular prism

5. sphere

6. cone

7. cylinder

8. cubes

9. cylinder

10. sphere

Page 133

Answers will vary

Page 134

1. a

2. c

3. c

4. b

Page 135

1.–6. Answers will vary

7. yes

8. no

9. no

10. yes

11. yes

12. yes

Page 136

Answers will vary

Page 137

Answers will vary

Page 138

1.

2.

3.

4.

5.

Page 139

Answers will vary

Page 140

1. 5:15

2. 9:30

3. 6:15

4. 10:30

5. 6:30

6. 11:15

7. 7:00

8. 4:15

9. 10:00

10. 3:30

11. 5:30

12. 12:00

13. 1:15

14. 2:30

15. 3:00

16. 7:30

17. 8:00

18. 1:00

19. 2:00

20. 9:15

21. 4:00

Answer Key *(cont.)*

Page 141

Part I

1. 7:30
2. 8:15
3. 9:00
4. 5:15
5. 12:00

Page 142

1. 2 hours
2. 1 hour
3. 3:45
4. 3 hours
5. 2:45
6. 2 hours

Page 143

Answers will vary

Page 144

1. $2\frac{1}{2}$ hours
2. 1 hour
3. reading class, because it is 2 hours long and music is only 1 hour
4. art class
5. math class
6. lunch

Page 145

Answers will vary

Page 146

1. blue jays and robins
2. mockingbirds
3. 15 blue jays
4. 20 total
5. 55 birds

Page 147

1. Panama City
2. 15 students
3. Myrtle Beach and Virginia Beach
4. 9 votes each
5. Cancun
6. 6 votes
7. 6 votes
8. 51 total votes

Page 148

Answers will vary

Page 149

1. years
2. centuries
3. decades
4. centuries
5. decades
6. centuries
7. years
8. years
9. decades
10. years
11. centuries
12. centuries
13. centuries
14. decades
15. years

Page 150

1. September 12, 2001
2. 2 years, 7 months
3. Survived being hit by a car and Graduated obedience school
4. August 10, 2003

Page 151

Answers will vary

Page 152

1. 1607
2. No one knows; it disappeared
3. Jamestown
4. The Pilgrims

Page 153

1. past
2. present
3. future
4. present
5. past
6. present
7. future
8. present

Page 154

Answers may vary

Page 155

Answers will vary

Page 156

1. 5   4. 2
2. 1   5. 4
3. 3

Page 157

Answers will vary

Page 158

1. False   6. True
2. False   7. True
3. True   8. False
4. False   9. False
5. False   10. False

Answer Key (cont.)

Page 159

Answers will vary

Page 160

Helpful:

1, 2, 3, 5, 6, 9

Page 161

Answers will vary

Page 162

(Some answers may vary)

1. They lived in settled homes; family members had certain chores
2. Taking care of the crops
3. A settled tribe because they raised crops and lived in permanent homes
4. Answers will vary
5. To hunt and get food

Page 163

1. c   4. a
2. b   5. b
3. c

Page 164

Answers will vary

Page 165

Page 166

1. Lake
2. Woods
3. Houses
4. River
5. Mountains
6. Train or railroad tracks
7. Road
8. Town or City

Page 167

Items to be colored:

a butter churn

an ax

a kettle/pot

a covered wagon

a coonskin hat

a plow

a spinning wheel

a wooden barrel

Page 168

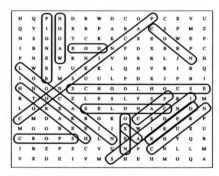

Page 169

1. The Cherokee Indians lived much like the white settlers around them.
2. Sequoyah
3. For expansion and gold had been found
4. Andrew Jackson
5. The Indian Removal Act

6. Oklahoma
7. They died along the way
8. The Trail of Tears
9. Because it was so sad that so many died and the way they were forced to leave
10. Answers will vary

Page 170

Answers will vary

Page 171

Answers will vary

Page 172

1. 13
2. England
3. Because of unending disagreements, and they did not like England making laws for them. They wanted to make their own law.
4. the Revolutionary War
5. Ben Franklin, Thomas Jefferson, Paul Revere (any 2)
6. Thomas Jefferson
7. It was a paper that declared to the world that the colonies wanted to be free from England.
8. July 4, 1776
9. America's birthday
10. Answers will vary

Page 173

1. True
2. False
3. True
4. False
5. True
6. False

Answer Key (cont.)

7. True

8. True

9. True

10. False

Page 174

1. She made the first flag

2. To represent the 13 colonies

3. George Washington helped Betsy Ross

4. There are more stars for all of the states

Page 175

1. The 50 stars represent the 50 states

2. The 13 stripes represent the original 13 colonies

3. Red, white, and blue

4. Answers will vary

Page 176

Answers will vary

Page 177

Answers will vary

Page 178

1. b

2. d

3. c

4. i

5. a

6. h

7. j

8. e

9. g

10. f

Page 179

Answers will vary

Page 180

Should be circled:

1, 3, 4, 6, 9

Page 181

Answers will vary

page 182

Answers will vary

Page 183

Answers will vary

Page 184

Answers will vary

Page 185

Answers will vary

Page 186

Answers will vary

Page 187

1. False

2. True

3. False

4. True

5. False

6. 4

7. 1

8. 2

9. 3

Page 188

environment

adapt

desert

water

food

sunlight

living

weather

protection

Page 189

Part II

1. flower

2. stem

3. roots

4. leaf

5. flower

6. roots

Page 190

1. i

2. a

3. b

4. g

5. h

6. j

7. c

8. f

9. e

10. d

Page 191

Answers will vary

Answer Key *(cont.)*

Page 192

Part I

1. I
2. L
3. I
4. I
5. L
6. I
7. L
8. I
9. L
10. L

Part II

Answers will vary

Page 193

1. o
2. h
3. h
4. c
5. c
6. h
7. h
8. h
9. h
10. h

Page 194

1. f
2. e
3. h
4. g
5. b
6. c
7. d
8. a
9.–16. Answers will vary

Page 195

1. b
2. a
3. b
4. b
5. a
6. a
7. b
8. a

Page 196

Answers will vary

Page 197

Answers will vary

Page 198

Answers will vary

Page 199

1. True   5. True
2. True   6. True
3. True   7. True
4. False   8. False

Page 200

Rocks that should have an X:

1, 4, 7, 9, and 10

Page 201

Answers will vary

Page 202

1. e
2. a
3. d
4. b
5. c

Page 203

Answers that should be colored

1, 3, 4, 5, 7

Page 204

1. evaporation
2. condensation
3. precipitation
4. runoff
5. 4
6. vapor
7. precipitation
8. (any 3) rain, snow, hail, sleet

9–10 Answers will vary

Page 205

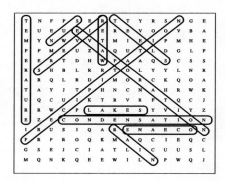

Page 206

Part I

Answers will vary

Part II

1. 24 hours
2. How the Earth is turned towards or away from the sun
3. sun
4. away

Answer Key (cont.)

Page 207

1. sunshine
2. moon
3. moon
4. sunshine
5. sunshine
6. moon
7. moon
8. sunshine

Page 208

1. a
2. a
3. b
4. b
5. a

Page 209

New moon, first quarter moon, full moon, last quarter moon

Page 210

Part I

Mercury, Venus, Earth, Mars, Jupiter, Saturn, Uranus, Neptune, Pluto

Part II

Answers will vary

Page 211

Part II

1. Mercury
2. Venus
3. Earth
4. Mars
5. Sun
6. Earth

Page 212

Part II

1. e
2. c
3. d
4. b
5. a

Page 213

Answers will vary

Page 214

Statements that should be colored:

2, 3, 5, 8, 9, 10, 11

Page 215

1. pull
2. push
3. pull
3. pull
4. push
5. push
6. push
7. push
8. push
9. push
10. push
11. pull

Page 216

1. a
2. b
3. b
4. a
5. b

Page 217

Objects that should be circled:

a nail, a paper clip, a metal washer, a metal fork, a metal bolt, another magnet

Page 218

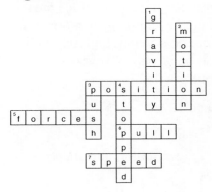

Page 219

1. liquid
2. gas
3. solid
4. liquid
5. gas
6. solid
7. solid
8. liquid
9. gas
10. liquid
11. liquid
12. solid
13. liquid
14. gas
15. solid

Answer Key (cont.)

Page 220

Answers will vary

Page 221

Objects that should be circled:
rock, computer, elephant, tree,
watermelon, grown woman,
ape, car, jug, gallon of ice cream,
lamp, keychain, grown dog,
camera, bowling ball, baseball
bat, boot, pair of scissors,
book, eagle

Page 222

1. properties

2. size, color, and shape

3. gas

4. liquid

5. solid

6. mass

7. weight

8. particles

Page 223

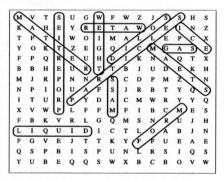